Success Strategies for College & Life

Second Edition

Kimberly Cunningham
Ashley Chance Fox

Bowling Green Community College
of Western Kentucky University

4050 Westmark Drive • P O Box 1840 • Dubuque IA 52004-1840

Cover image © Aubrey Beard

Kendall Hunt
publishing company

www.kendallhunt.com
Send all inquiries to:
4050 Westmark Drive
Dubuque, IA 52004-1840

Copyright © 2008, 2009 by Kimberly Cunningham and Ashley Chance Fox

ISBN 978-0-7575-6279-2

Kendall/Hunt Publishing Company has the exclusive rights to reproduce this work,
to prepare derivative works from this work, to publicly distribute this work,
to publicly perform this work and to publicly display this work.

All rights reserved. No part of this publication may be reproduced,
stored in a retrieval system, or transmitted, in any form or by any
means, electronic, mechanical, photocopying, recording, or otherwise,
without the prior written permission of the copyright owner.

Printed in the United States of America
10 9 8 7 6 5 4 3 2 1

Contents

Letter of Welcome from Dr. Sherry Reid, Dean Bowling Green Community College   v

Letter of Welcome from University Experience Coordinators, Ashley Chance Fox and Kimberly Cunningham   vii

Acknowledgments   ix

Section 1: Bowling Green Community College   1

Chapter 1: History, Traditions, and Academics   3
- BGCC History   3
- BGCC Mission and Vision   3
- The Western Creed   4
- Preston Student Success Center   6
- Academic Advising   6
- Alice Rowe Learning Assistance Center   6
- University Experience 175C   6
- General Education and Your Major   7
- Financial Aid Checklist   7
- Courses Meeting Revised WKU General Education Requirements Offered on South Campus (2009–2010)   8
- Majors Available at South Campus   9
- WKU Bookstore at South Campus   11
- Parking and Transportation   10
- Websites and Links   11
- Important Telephone Numbers   11
- WKU Student Handbook   12

Section 2: College Success Strategies   13

Chapter 2: Understanding Motivation   15

Chapter 3: Managing Time and Money   29

Chapter 4: Test Taking   49

Chapter 5: Taking Notes, Writing, and Speaking   73

Section 3: Career Development   93

Chapter 6: Career Services   95

Section 4: Library and Technology   111

Chapter 7: Library Skills   113

Chapter 8: Technology Resources   125

A Leading American University with International Reach

Dear Student,

Welcome to Bowling Green Community College of Western Kentucky University and to your special section of University Experience. This course was designed to help you take full advantage of the opportunities you will enjoy as a beginning college student and to guide you as you face and conquer the challenges associated with this dynamic time in your life. The mission of Bowling Green Community College and the primary goal of this course is to equip you with the knowledge and skills you need to achieve confidence, independence, and academic success.

Throughout your first semester, you will continue to learn about yourself, the campus, and academic life. You will strengthen your study skills and gain valuable information that will assist you in making critical professional and career development decisions. Additionally, you will be introduced to and become familiar with resources and services available to answer your questions and enhance your emotional, intellectual, and social growth. As a BGCC student, you will have access to the Preston Student Success Center that provides enrollment services, learning assistance, and a state-of-the-art computer lab. I strongly encourage you to take advantage of this beneficial resource.

Because some of the most valuable learning occurs outside the classroom, we hope you will accept the invitation to engage in the numerous educational, social, and recreational activities taking place on "the hill" and at the South Campus. Finally, as a WKU/BGCC student, you will be persuaded to seek opportunities that broaden your knowledge and facilitate your contributions to society through meaningful community service and civic engagement.

I am very glad that you have chosen to attend Bowling Green Community College, and I sincerely hope that you will find your experience here one that fulfills your expectations and lays a strong foundation for a successful academic career.

Sincerely

Sherry M. Reid

Sherry Reid
Dean

The Spirit Makes the Master
Bowling Green Community College | 2355 Nashville Road, Suite B | Bowling Green, KY 42101-1094

A LEADING AMERICAN UNIVERSITY WITH INTERNATIONAL REACH

Dear University Experience Student,

Welcome to the Bowling Green Community College of Western Kentucky University and to University Experience. This is an exciting time for you as you begin your journey into Higher Education. During your first semester you will have new experiences, meet new people and have new freedoms and responsibilities that you have never had before. University Experience will assist you in your transition and will teach you about WKU history and campus, academic success skills, navigating the library, and social responsibilities.

Our campus is full of knowledgeable, caring, helpful and supportive faculty and staff. We have high expectations for you and your academic achievements. To help you in your academic success the Bowling Green Community College offers programs and services such as: the A.C.E.S. Living and Learning Communities, tutoring in the Alice Rowe Learning Assistance Center, the First Year Foundations Program, and the Women in Transition Program (for "non-traditional" female students) to name a few.

Your University Experience Instructor, no matter whom you are lucky enough to take, is dedicated to first-year students and their success. You could not have asked for a more devoted and enthusiastic instructor! Our goals are to help you with the skills needed to be academically successful and transition smoothly through your first year.

We again offer a warm welcome to BGCC and University Experience. If there is anything we can do to help you with your experience here, please do not hesitate to ask us (or your University Experience instructor). We also wish you a fantastic first year at Bowling Green Community College of Western Kentucky University. GO TOPS!

Sincerely,

Ashley Chance Fox
Coordinator of University Experience

Kimberly Cunningham
Coordinator of the A.C.E.S. Living and Learning Communities

The Spirit Makes the Master

Bowling Green Community College | 2355 Nashville Road, Suite B | Bowling Green, KY 42101-1094

Acknowledgments

The University Experience Coordinators would like to thank the following people, without whose help this project would never have been completed: The Bowling Green Community College and Western Kentucky University faculty and staff who have been tremendously helpful and supportive. A special thanks to Dr. Sherry Reid, Stephanie Hooker, Aron London, Sara McCaslin, Elizabeth Heller, Jack Moeller, and Mary Ann Bokkon. Thanks to Aubrey Beard for her fantastic work with the photographs.

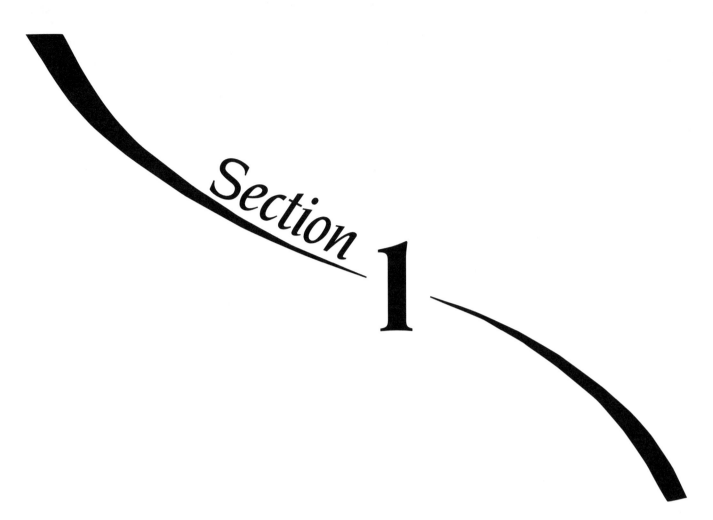

Section 1

Bowling Green Community College

History, Traditions, and Academics

Chapter 1

Bowling Green Community College (BGCC) was established in 1986 to expand the educational opportunities in the community and the region. The Community College is one of the five undergraduate colleges within Western Kentucky University.

The mission of the Community College is to expand educational opportunities in the community and in the region. BGCC is located on the WKU South Campus on Nashville Road in Bowling Green, Kentucky.

Bowling Green Community College offers students a choice from more than 20 different Programs, Certificates and two-year Associate Degrees through its Arts and Sciences, Business and Computer Studies, and Health Sciences Divisions.

BGCC History

- The Early Years . . . under the direction of Carl Chelf
- The Brick House Years . . . under the direction of Jerry Boles
- The Relocation Years . . . under the direction of L. Paul Rice
- Ribbon Cutting and Grand Opening of South Campus Facility
- The Growing Years . . . under the direction of Frank Conley
- The Years of Growth and Change . . . under the direction of Dr. Sherry Reid

BGCC Mission and Vision

As one of the six undergraduate colleges of Western Kentucky University, Bowling Green Community College supports the University's vision by aspiring to be recognized as one of the best community colleges in Kentucky.

BGCC supports the WKU mission by offering to its constituents:

- An open admissions policy
- An inclusive, student-centered environment
- Strong academic support courses and services
- Associate degree programs focused on career-oriented curricula
- Associate degree programs focused on transfer to baccalaureate institutions
- Lifelong learning opportunities
- Educational opportunities in support of economic and workforce development

BGCC Values

- Open access to quality educational opportunities
- Student success through individual attention
- Excellence in teaching, advising, and supporting students
- High quality programs and services through continuous improvement in academic and administrative processes
- The intellectual, professional, and personal growth of students, faculty, and staff

The Western Creed

Western Kentucky University is a community dedicated to learning, where ideas are offered, examined, and discussed.

As a member of this community, I have both a personal and shared responsibility to participate actively in university life by:

Practicing personal and academic integrity:

Seeking unity by respecting the dignity of all persons:

Celebrating and embracing diversity:

Encouraging freedom of expression:

Acting in accordance with basic principles of citizenship:

Preserving and appreciating the natural beauty of the campus:

Enriching all aspects of life through the educational process:
and by

Embracing the ideals expressed on the university seal:
"Life More Life" and "The Spirit Makes the Master,"
by pursuing personal growth and a life of excellence.

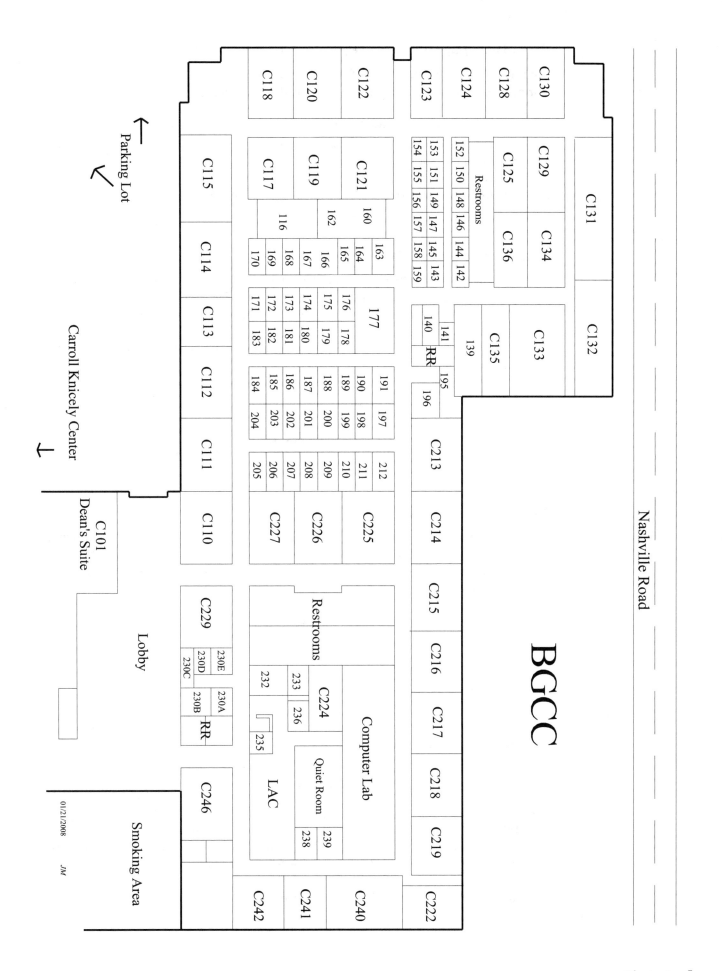

Preston Student Success Center

The PSSC is located in the heart of the Bowling Green Community College. It consists of four distinct areas and offers services such as the following:

- Alice Rowe Learning Assistance Center (free tutoring services)
- Enrollment and Advising Services (advising and registration)
- Open Computer Lab
- University Experience Classes and Faculty
- Visits from representatives from Financial Aid, Career Services, Counseling and Campus Activities

Academic Advising

During orientation each student will meet with an Academic Advisor who will help him/her plan a schedule and register via TopNet for classes. The student will be able to access his/her class schedule online through TopNet and will receive a copy of his/her summary class schedule today.

Each student attending Bowling Green Community College is assigned a full-time faculty member as an Academic Advisor to assist the student in planning a successful academic program. The Office of Enrollment Services also provides year round academic advising services for students of the College and can be found in the Preston Student Success Center.

Before enrolling in classes every semester, each student is required to contact his/her Advisor to schedule an appointment for academic advising, which ensures each student is placed in classes for his/her proposed degree program.

Alice Rowe Learning Assistance Center

The Alice Rowe Learning Assistance Center (LAC) is part of the Preston Student Success Center at the Bowling Green Community College. The primary goal of the LAC is to provide students with the resources they need in order to become successful, independent learners. Some of the services available to students include the following:

- Tutoring services (no appointment necessary)
- Academic Computer Lab with internet access
- Reserved reference materials
- Telecourse videos (for on-site viewing)
- Quiet study room

The LAC is a dynamic center, and the staff are proud to be a part of the overall mission of the Bowling Green Community College.

University Experience 175C

University Experience's mission is to support the academic, social, and moral development of first-year students and students in transition, and to help build and sustain a climate on campus that values intellectual curiosity, critical thinking, self awareness, caring about others, personal responsibility, leadership, hard work, and integrity.

This course is required for all new freshmen and transfer students with fewer than 24 hours of college credit. University Experience has many excellent qualities for new students, such as:

- ▲ Learning to use the WKU Libraries . . . ONLINE!
- ▲ Improving your study and test taking skills
- ▲ Improving your time management skills
- ▲ Providing opportunity to work in groups to get to know other new students
- ▲ Attending WKU activities and events . . . and getting credit for it in class!

General Education and Your Major

Depending on the major you choose, you may or may not be required to complete 44 hours of general education.

- ▲ 4-year majors (Bachelor Degree Programs)
  require that students complete 44 hours of general education plus all courses required in the major in order to graduate
- ▲ 2-year majors (Associate Degree Programs)
  do not require that students complete all 44 hours of general education in order to graduate

Therefore it is important to know the requirements for your major before registering for classes. You can easily find the classes required for your major by going to WKU's webpage (www.wku.edu) and selecting Academics. Then you will need to select undergraduate programs. Once on this page you will find an alphabetical list of all the degree programs offered at Western Kentucky University. Select your degree program, and you will find a list of curriculum required for your major, such as a suggested first semester, as well as, the general education requirements for your degree program.

Financial Aid Checklist

- ▲ Apply for 4-digit FAFSA PIN at www.fafsa.ed.gov. Parents of dependent students will also need a PIN.
- ▲ File the FAFSA at www.fafsa.ed.gov, using the appropriate year 1040 tax form. **You are not finished until you click "Submit My FAFSA Now"** *and* **see an EFC number.** The priority deadline is March 15 for the next school year, but you may file after that date. Info hotline 1-800-433-3243.
- ▲ You will receive a Student Aid Report (SAR) within 2 weeks, which indicates whether you must do Verification. You can make corrections at www.fafsa.ed.gov.
- ▲ Within 2–4 weeks, the FAFSA Processing Center will forward your information to WKU. At that point, students are placed into one of two groups:

  A) We will notify via email the approximately 33 percent of students selected to complete Verification. If you are in this group, you will need to submit a Verification Worksheet, available at http://www.wku.edu/Info/FinAid/faforms.htm, along with signed copies of the 1040s you used to complete the FAFSA. The verification process typically takes 2–4 weeks.

  OR

  B) The remaining 66 percent of students not selected do not have to complete this step.
- ▲ Students beginning at WKU in the Spring, Winter, or Summer term will visit http://www.wku.edu/Info/FinAid/faforms.htm to complete the appropriate Winter/Spring/Summer Application. Once all of the above steps are completed **AND** you have registered for classes, the Financial Aid Office will build an aid package for you. This package may include Pell grants, CAP grants, Stafford loans, KEES estimates, Parent PLUS loans, etc. and is largely dependent on your EFC. We will send a message to your WKU email account when you have been awarded.

▲ You can view this offer and choose to accept or decline the aid in your TopNet account. Select "Financial Aid," "Award," then "Accept Award." It is very important to check "Account Summary by Term" near the start of the semester. This screen shows your WKU bill and payment credits. A positive bottom line number indicates the amount of money you currently owe to WKU, while $0 or a negative balance indicates the bill is paid. If you believe there is an error, please contact us.

▲ **If this is your first time taking out a Stafford student loan,** please visit www.kheaa.com and complete "Entrance Loan Counseling" and "E-Sign My MPN" in the upper right-hand corner of the page. You will need your FAFSA PIN to sign.

Please be aware that it is your responsibility to respond to letters and emails regarding your financial aid. Simply completing the FAFSA does not guarantee financial assistance, but it is the first step in the process. We look forward to working with you!
—WKU Student Financial Assistance, (270) 745-2755

Outreach Counselor: Mary Ann Bokkon, (270) 745-5162, mary.bokkon@wku.edu, extended campus locations and dates at http://calendar.yahoo.com/mary_bokkon.

Courses Meeting Revised WKU General Education Requirements Offered on South Campus (2009–2010)

CATEGORY A: ORGANIZATION AND COMMUNICATION OF IDEAS
(12 hours/4 courses required)

I. Freshman English (ENGL 100C) (Required)

   Junior English (ENG 300) (Required but NOT available on South Campus)

II. Foreign Language (Students who enrolled in 200420 and thereafter are required to complete the second semester level or higher to fulfill this requirement.)

   Pre 200420 students may take any 1 semester of F.L. to meet the requirement.
   ▲ Spanish (SPN 101C)
   ▲ Spanish (SPN 102C) (For students with 2 yrs. H.S. Spanish)
   ▲ French (FRN 101C)
   ▲ French (FRN 102C)
   ▲ German (GRM 101C)

III. Public Speaking (3 hours required)
   ▲ Fundamentals of Public Speaking (SPCH 145C)
   ▲ Business and Professional Speaking (SPCH 161C)

CATEGORY B: HUMANITIES
(9 hours/3 courses required)

I. Introduction to Literature (ENGL 200C) (Must have completed ENGL 100C)
II. Electives (Choose *two* courses representing two different fields of study)
   ▲ Art Appreciation (ARTS 100C)
   ▲ Music Appreciation (MUSI 120C)
   ▲ New Testament (RLST 100C)
   ▲ Old Testament (RLST 101C)
   ▲ Introduction to Religious Studies (RLST 102C)

CATEGORY C: SOCIAL AND BEHAVIORAL SCIENCES
(9 hours/3 courses required)

I. Western Civilization (HIST 119C or HIST 120C) (Required)

II. Electives (Choose *two* courses representing two different fields of study.)
- Introduction to Leadership Studies (LEA 200C)
- Introduction to Psychology (PSYC 100C)
- Developmental Psychology (PSYC 199C)
- Introduction to Economics (ECO 150C)
- Principles of Economics—Micro (ECO 202C)
- Principles of Economics—Macro (ECO 203C)
- Introduction to Sociology (SOC 100C)
- Marriage and Family (SOC 220C)
- American National Government (GOV 110)
- Principles of Human Geography (GEO 101C)
- Women's Studies (WMN 200C)

CATEGORY D: NATURAL SCIENCES AND MATHEMATICS
(9 hours/3 courses required)

I. Science (9 to 10 hours—at least *two* fields must be represented and at least one lab experience must be included.)
- General Biology (BIO 113C) Lab Experience (BIO 114C)
- Human Anatomy and Physiology (BIO 131C—Lecture and Lab sections)
- General Microbiology (BIO 207C) (Lab BIOL 208—Main Campus)
- Introduction to Chemistry (CHM 101C—Includes lab experience)
- Chemistry for Health Sciences (CHM 109C)
- Introduction to Man's Physical Environment (GEO 100C)

II. Mathematics (3 hours)
- General Mathematics (MA 109C) (No test score or prereq required)
- College Algebra (MA 116C) (MPE or MA 100C required)
- Trigonometry (MA 117C)

CATEGORY E: WORLD CULTURES AND AMERICAN CULTURAL DIVERSITY
(3 hours/1 course required)

- African American Studies (AFA 190C)
- Cultural Diversity in the United States (FOLK 280C)
- World Regional Geography (GEO 110C)

CATEGORY F: HEALTH AND WELLNESS
(2 to 3 hours–two 1 hour PE activity classes or one 2 to 3 hour course required)

- Human Nutrition (CFSC 111C)—3 hours
- Personal Health (HED 100C)—3 hours
- Drug Abuse (HED 165C)—3 hours
- Personal Adjustment (PSYC 250C)—3 hours
- Life Fitness and Wellness (PED 100C)—3 hours
- Physical Education Activity Classes (PED 101C)—1 hour each
- Military Mountaineering and Leadership (MILS 101C)—2 hours

Majors Available at South Campus
BUSINESS DIVISION
Business Technology—288
    With concentrations in:
        Management Information Systems

    Manufacturing Management
    Office Management
    Real Estate
    Business Management
    Banking
    Retail Management
    Management (Prep)—2+2 Program
Hospitality Management—245
Information Systems Technology—223
Office Systems Technology—291
Paralegal (Seeking Admission)—276P
Paralegal (Admitted)—276
Pre-Gordon Ford College of Business—185
Real Estate Certificate—195

LIBERAL ARTS AND SCIENCES

Associates in Interdisciplinary Studies—256
Interdisciplinary Early Childhood Education—248
Not Pursuing a Degree—297
Pre-College of Arts and Letters—183
Pre-College of Education and Behavioral Sciences—187
Pre-College of Health and Human Services—171
Pre-College of Science and Technology—170
Undeclared—181

HEALTH SCIENCE

Healthcare Information Systems (Seeking Admission)—261P
Healthcare Information Systems (Admitted)—261
Nursing (Seeking Admission)—273P
Nursing (Admitted)—273
Paramedicine (Seeking Admission)—265P
Pre-College of Health and Human Services—171

WKU Bookstore at South Campus

You can go online to reserve your textbooks, check textbook prices, and see items available at the bookstore. Information you will need to reserve your books can be found on your class schedule, so please have this available when reserving books online or purchasing books on campus at the bookstore.

    To reserve/purchase books online, please visit the following link: http://www.bookstore.wku.edu/

Parking and Transportation

A commuter parking permit is required to park in the South Campus lot. No parking is allowed by students in the Carroll Knicely Visitor Parking area. Also, behind the Bowling Green Community College there is a Campbell Lane Parking area which is available for use. This lot requires either the Campbell Lane Park & Ride Permit or any other parking permit issued at Western Kentucky University.

    Please visit the Parking and Transportation website for purchase prices on permits. Parking permits can be purchased online through Parking and Transportation at the following link: https://wkuparking.t2systems.com/cmn/auth.aspx

Please remember, if you order the permit online by a date specified on the Parking and Transportation website, the permit can be mailed to you. However, permits purchased for the spring and after the priority deadline for the fall will have to be picked up at the Parking and Transportation office located between the Campbell Lane Lot and South Campus, next to the Hattie L. Preston Intramural Sports Complex.

Shuttle services are available at South Campus, which will allow for transportation to classes on Main Campus or various other locations. For more information on shuttle services, please visit see the BGCC website and click on Student Services.

Websites and Links

Alice Rowe Learning Assistance Center	http://www.bgcc.wku.edu/LearningAssistanceCenter.htm
Blackboard	https://ecourses.wku.edu/
Bowling Green Community College	http://www.bgcc.wku.edu/
CAB	http://www.wku.edu/cab/
Campus Directory	https://acsapps.wku.edu/pls/prod/dirpkg.prompt
Health Services	http://www.wku.edu/healthservices/
Office of Distance Learning	http://www.wku.edu/reachu/
Preston Student Success Center	http://www.bgcc.wku.edu/PSSC.html
Student Activities and Organizations	http://www.wku.edu/Dept/Support/StuAffairs/SAUC/index.htm
Student Disability Services	http://www.wku.edu/Dept/Support/AcadAffairs/SDS/sds.htm
Student Services	http://www.wku.edu/Dept/Support/StuAffairs/
TopNet	http://topnet.wku.edu/
Webmail	https://mail.wku.edu/
Western Kentucky University	http://www.wku.edu/
WKU Events Calendar	http://www.wku.edu/Info/Events/

Important Telephone Numbers

Alice Rowe Learning Assistance Center	(270) 780-2536
Bowling Green Community College	(270) 780-2550
Career Services	(270) 745-3095
Counseling Services	(270) 745-3159
Disability Services	(270) 745-5004
Financial Aid	(270) 745-2755
IT Help Desk	(270) 745-7000
Health Services	(270) 745-5641
Parking/Transportation	(270) 745-2361
Preston Center	(270) 745-5217
South Campus Bookstore	(270) 780-2525
WKU Police	(270) 745-2548

In compliance with the Americans with Disabilities Act, it is the student's responsibility to contact their instructor concerning any special accommodations. **If you need any special assistance and have filled out all the paperwork through Western Kentucky University's Office of Student Disability Services, please see your instructor so they can accommodate your needs. If you need to contact the Office of Student Disability Services please call (270) 745-5004.** Please do not request accommodations without the proper ADA paperwork.

WKU Student Handbook

Students attending Bowling Green Community College are also WKU students and must follow all WKU guidelines for student behavior as outlined in the WKU Student Handbook. To access the handbook online, please go to the following link: http://www.wku.edu/handbook/current/.

Section 2

College Success Strategies

Understanding Motivation

Chapter 2

Chapter Focus

Read to answer these key questions:

What do I want from college?   What is the value of a college education?   How do I choose my major and career?   How can I motivate myself to be successful?   How can I begin habits that lead to success?   How is persistence a key to success?

Most students attend college with dreams of making their lives better. Some students are there to explore interests and possibilities, and others have more defined career goals. Being successful in college and attaining your dreams begins with motivation. It provides the energy or drive to find your direction and to reach your goals. Without motivation, it is difficult to accomplish anything.

Not everyone is successful in college. As a freshman in college, I attended an orientation in which I was told to look at the student to the left and the student to the right of me. The speaker said that one of us would not make it through the freshman year. I remember telling myself that the speaker must have been talking about one of the other two students and not me. That was the beginning of my motivation to be successful in college. Unfortunately about one-third of college students drop out in the first year. Forty percent of students who start college do not finish their degree. Having a good understanding of your gifts and talents, reasons for attending college, career goals, and how to motivate yourself will help you to reach your dreams.

What Do I Want from College?

Succeeding in college requires time and effort. You will have to give up some of your time spent on leisure activities and working. You will give up some time spent with your friends and families. Making sacrifices and working hard is easier if you know what you want to achieve through your efforts. One of the first steps in motivating yourself to be successful in college is to have a clear and specific understanding of your reasons for attending college. Are you attending college as a way to obtain a satisfying career? Is financial security one of your goals? Will you feel more satisfied if you are living up to your potential? What are your hopes and dreams, and how will college help you to achieve your goals?

When you are having difficulties or doubts about your ability to finish your college education, remember your hopes and dreams and your plans for the future. It is a good idea to write these ideas down, think about them, and revise them from time to time. Complete the exercise "What Do I Want from College?" located at the end of this chapter.

From *College & Career Success*, 3rd edition by Marsha Fralick. Copyright © 2006 by Kendall/Hunt Publishing Company. Reprinted by permission.

What Is the Value of a College Education?

Many college students say that getting a satisfying job that pays well and achieving financial security are important reasons for attending college. By going to college you can get a job that pays more per hour. You can work fewer hours to earn a living and have more time for leisure activities. You can spend your time at work doing something that you like to do. A report issued by the Census Bureau in 2002 listed the following education and income statistics for all races and both genders throughout the United States.[1] Lifetime income assumes that a person works thirty years before retirement.

Average Earnings Based on Education Level

Education	Yearly Income	Lifetime Income
High school graduate	$30,400	$1,226,575
Some college, no degree	$36,800	$1,494,989
Associate degree	$38,200	$1,563,702
Bachelor's degree	$52,200	$2,140,864
Master's degree	$62,300	$2,463,059
Professional degree	$109,600	$4,411,542

Notice that income rises with the educational level. A person with a bachelor's degree earns almost twice as much as a high school graduate. Of course these are average figures across the nation. Some individuals earn higher or lower salaries. People have assumed that you would certainly be rich if you were a millionaire. College won't make you an instant millionaire, but over a lifetime you earn over a million and a half dollars by having an associate's degree. People fantasize about winning the lottery. The reality is that the probability of winning the lottery is very low. In the long run, you have a better chance of improving your financial status by going to college.

Let's do some further comparisons. A high school graduate earns an average of $1,226,575 over a lifetime. A college graduate with a bachelor's degree earns $2,140,864 over a lifetime. A college graduate earns $914,289 more than a high school graduate does over a lifetime. So how much is a college degree worth? It is worth $914,289 over a lifetime. Would you go to college if someone offered to pay you $914,289? Here are some more interesting figures we can derive from the table above:

Completing one college course is worth $22,857.
($914,289 divided by 40 courses in a bachelor's degree)

Going to class for one hour is worth $476.
($22,857 divided by 48 hours in a semester class)

Would you take a college class if someone offered to pay you $22,857? Would you go to class today for one hour if someone offered to pay you $476? Of course, if this sounds too good to be true, remember that you will receive these "payments" over a working lifetime of thirty years.

Money is only one of the values of going to college. Can you think of other reasons to attend college? Here are some less tangible reasons . . .

- College helps you to develop your potential.
- College opens the door to many satisfying careers.
- College prepares you to be an informed citizen and fully participate in the democratic process.
- College increases your understanding and widens your view of the world.

- College allows you to participate in a conversation with the great minds of all times and places. For example, reading the work of Plato is like having a conversation with that famous philosopher. You can continue great conversations with your faculty and fellow students.
- College helps to increase your confidence, self-esteem, and self-respect.

> What is the value of a college education to you?

Choosing a Major and Career

Having a definite major and career choice is a good motivation for completing your college education. It is difficult to put in the work necessary to be successful if you do not have a clear picture of your future career; however, three out of four college students are undecided about their major. For students who have chosen a major, 30 to 75 percent of a graduating class will change that major two or more times.[2] Unclear or indefinite career goals are some of the most significant factors that identify students at risk of dropping out of college.[3] Students often drop out or extend their stay in college because they are uncertain about their major or want to change their major. Choosing an appropriate college major is one of the most difficult and important decisions that college students can make.

How do people choose a career? There are many complex factors that go into your career choice. This course will help you to become aware of these factors and to think critically about them in order to make a good choice about your career. Some of the factors involved in choosing a career include

Heredity. You inherit genes from your parents that play a role in shaping who you are.

Intelligence. Every person has a unique mixture of talents and skills. You can work to develop these skills.

Experience. Your experiences can either build your self-confidence or cause you to doubt your abilities.

Environment. What careers have you observed in your environment? Maybe your father was a doctor and you grew up familiar with careers in medicine. Your parents may have encouraged you to choose a particular career. You may want to learn about other possibilities.

Social roles. Maybe you learned that men are engineers and women are teachers because your father is an engineer and your mother is a teacher. It is important to think critically about traditional roles so that your choices are not limited.

Learning. What you have learned will play a part in your career decision. You may need to learn new behaviors and establish new habits.

Learning Style. Knowing how you like to learn can help you be successful in college as well as on the job. Your learning style may provide options for selecting a career as well.

Relationships. We sometimes choose careers to enhance relationships. For example, you may choose a career that gives you time to spend with your family or with people who are important to you.

Stress. Our ability to cope with stress plays a part in career choice. Some enjoy challenges; others value peace of mind.

Health. Good health increases career options and enjoyment of life.

Factors in Career Choice[4]

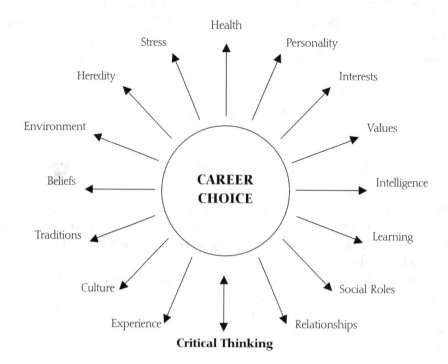

Personality. Your personality is a major factor influencing which career you might enjoy.

Values. What you value determines which career you will find satisfying.

Culture. Your culture has an influence on which careers you value.

Traditions. Traditions often guide career choice.

Beliefs. Your beliefs about yourself and the world determine your behavior and career choice.

Interests. If you choose a career that matches your interests, you can find satisfaction in your career.

How can you choose the major that is best for you? The best way is to first understand yourself; become aware of your personality traits, learning style, interests, preferred lifestyle, values, gifts, and talents. The next step is to do career research to determine the career that best matches your personal characteristics. Next, plan your education to prepare for your career. Here are some questions to answer to help you understand yourself and what career and major would be best for you.

To learn about yourself, explore these areas:

- **What is my personality type?** Psychologists have studied personality types and career choice. Assessing your personality type will give you some general ideas about careers that will give you satisfaction.
- **What is my learning style?** Being aware of your learning style will help you identify learning strategies that work best for you. Knowing how you learn best can help you identify your gifts and talents and find a career that matches them.
- **What are my interests?** Knowing about your interests is important in choosing a satisfying career.

- **What kind of lifestyle do I prefer?** Think about how you want to balance work, leisure, and family.
- **What are my values?** Knowing what you value (what is most important to you) will help you make good decisions about your life.

To learn about career possibilities, research the following:

- **What career matches my personality, interests, aptitudes and values?** Learn how to do career research to find the best career for you. Find a career that has a good outlook for the future.
- **How can I plan my education to get the career I want?** Once you have identified your area of interest, consult your college catalog or advisor to make an educational plan that matches your career goals.

By following the above steps, you can find the major that is best for you and minimize the time you spend in college.

Answer one of the following:
- ☞ If you have chosen a major, why is it the best major for you?
- ☞ If you haven't chosen a major yet, what are some steps in choosing the right major and career?

How to Be Motivated

There are many ways to be motivated.

- You can **improve your concentration** and motivation for studying by managing your external and internal distractions.
- You can be motivated by internal or external factors called **intrinsic or extrinsic motivation**.
- You can become aware of your **locus of control**, or where you place the responsibility for control over your life. If you are in control, you are more likely to be motivated to succeed.
- You can join a club, organization, or athletic team. **Affiliation motivation** involves taking part in school activities that increase your motivation to stay in college.
- **Achievement** and competition are motivating to some students.
- You can **apply the principles of learning** and use positive reinforcement as a motivation to establish desirable behaviors.

Let's examine each type of motivation in more detail and see if some of these ideas can be useful to you.

Improving Your Concentration

Have you ever watched lion tamers concentrate? If their attention wanders, they are likely to become the lion's dinner. Skilled athletes, musicians, and artists don't have any trouble concentrating. They are motivated to concentrate. Think about a time when you were totally focused on what you were doing. You were motivated to continue. You can improve your concentration and motivation for studying by managing your external and internal distractions.

Manage your external environment. Your environment will either help you to study or distract you from studying. We are all creatures of habit. If you try to study in front of the TV, you will watch TV because that is what you are accustomed to doing in front of the TV. If you study in bed, you will fall asleep because your body associates the bed with sleeping. If you study in the kitchen, you will eat. Find an environment that minimizes distractions. One idea is to study in the library. In the library, there are many cues that tell you to study. There are books and learning resources and other people studying. It will be easier to concentrate in that environment.

You may be able to set up a learning environment in your home. Find a place where you can place a desk or table, your computer, and your materials for learning. When you are in this place, use it for learning and studying only. When you are studying, focus on studying. Make it a habit to study in this place. When you are relaxing, go somewhere else and focus on relaxing.

Because of past experiences and learning, our environment has a powerful influence on our behavior. Choose the right environment for what you are doing. Don't confuse yourself by trying to study in front of the TV! Don't ruin your enjoyment of TV by trying to study while watching it. When you are relaxing, focus on relaxing and don't worry about studying. When you are studying, focus on studying and don't get distracted thinking about relaxing.

> **MANAGING INTERNAL DISTRACTIONS**
> – Be here now
> – Spider technique
> – Worry time
> – Checkmark technique
> – Increase activity
> – Find an incentive
> – Change topics

Manage your internal distractions. Many of our distractions come from within. Here are some techniques for managing these internal distractions:

1. Be here now.
Choose where you will place your attention. If you are in a lecture and you begin to think about eating cookies, notice that you are thinking about cookies and bring your attention back to the lecture. You can tell yourself, "Be here now." If you try to force yourself not to think about cookies, you will think about them even more. Just notice when your attention has drifted away and choose to bring it gently back to where you want it. This will take some practice since attention tends to wander often.

2. The spider technique.
If you hold a tuning fork to a spider web, the web vibrates and the spider senses that it has caught a tasty morsel and goes seeking the food. After awhile, the spider discovers that there is no food and learns to ignore the vibrations caused by the tuning fork. When you are sitting in the library studying and someone walks in talking and laughing, you can choose to pay attention either to the distraction or to studying. Decide to continue to pay attention to studying.

3. Set up a worry time.
Many times worries interfere with concentration. Some people have been successful in setting up a worry time. Here's how it works:

- Set a specific time each day for worrying.
- When worries distract you from your studies, remind yourself that you have set aside time for worrying.
- Tell yourself, "Be here now."
- Keep your worry appointment.
- During your worry time, try to find some solutions or take some steps to resolve the things that cause you to worry.

4. Use the checkmark technique.
When you find yourself distracted from a lecture or from studying, place a checkmark on a piece of paper and refocus your attention on the task at hand. You will find that your checkmarks decrease over time.

5. Increase your activity.
Take a break. Stretch and move. Read and listen actively by asking questions about the material and answering them as you read or listen.

6. Find an incentive or reward.
Tell yourself that when you finish, you will do something enjoyable.

7. Change topics.
Changing study topics may help you to concentrate and avoid fatigue.

> What concentration techniques can help you be more motivated, and study more effectively?

Intrinsic or Extrinsic Motivation

Intrinsic motivation comes from within. It means that you do an activity because you enjoy it or find personal meaning in it. With intrinsic motivation, the nature of the activity itself or the consequences of the activity motivate you. For example, let's say that I am interested in learning to play the piano. I am motivated to practice playing the piano because I like the sound of the piano and feel very satisfied when I can play music that I enjoy. I practice because I like to practice, not because I have to practice. When I get tired or frustrated, I work through it or put it aside and come back to it because I want to learn to play the piano well.

You can be intrinsically motivated to continue in college because you enjoy learning and find the college experience satisfying. Look for ways to enjoy college and to find some personal satisfaction in it. If you enjoy college, it becomes easier to do the work required to be successful. Think about what you say to yourself about college. If you are saying negative things such as, "I don't want to be here," it will be difficult to continue.

Extrinsic motivation comes as a result of an external reward from someone else. Examples of extrinsic rewards are certificates, bonuses, money, praise, and recognition. Taking the piano example again, let's say that I want my child to play the piano. The child does not know if he or she would like to play the piano. I give the child a reward for practicing the piano. I could pay the child for practicing or give praise for doing a good job. There are two possible outcomes of the extrinsic reward. After awhile, the child may gain skills and confidence and come to enjoy playing the piano. The extrinsic reward is no longer necessary because the child is now intrinsically motivated. Or the child may decide that he or she does not like to play the piano. The extrinsic reward is no longer effective in motivating the child to play the piano.

You can use extrinsic rewards to motivate yourself to be successful in college. Remind yourself of the payoff for getting a college degree: earning more money, having a satisfying career, being able to purchase a car and a house. Extrinsic rewards can be a first step in motivating yourself to attend college. With experience and achievement, you may come to like going to college and may become intrinsically motivated to continue your college education.

If you use intrinsic motivation to achieve your goal, you will be happier and more successful. If you do something like playing the piano because you enjoy it, you are more likely to spend the time necessary to practice to achieve your goal. If you view college as something that you enjoy and as valuable to you, it is easier to spend the time to do the required studying. When you get tired or frustrated, tell yourself that you are doing a good job (praise yourself) and think of the positive reasons that you want to get a college education.

1. What are your instrinsic motivations for going to college? Remember, intrinsic motivators are those you do because you enjoy them or they are personally meaningful.
2. What are your extrinsic motivators for going to college? Remember, extrinsic motivators are external rewards from someone else.

Locus of Control

Being aware of the concept of locus of control is another way of understanding motivation. The word *locus* means place. Locus of control is where you place the responsibility for control over your life. In other words, who is in charge? If you place the responsibility on yourself and believe that you have control over your life, you have internal locus of control. If you place the responsibility on others and think that luck or fate determines your future, you have external locus of control. Some people use internal or external locus of control in combination or favor one type in certain situations. If you favor an internal locus of control, you believe that to a great extent your actions determine your future. Studies have shown that students who use an internal locus of control are likely to have higher achievement in college.[5] The characteristics of students with internal and external locus of control are listed below.

Students with an internal locus of control

- believe that they are in control of their lives.
- understand that grades are directly related to the amount of study invested.
- are self-motivated.
- learn from their mistakes by figuring out what went wrong and how to fix the problem.
- think positively and try to make the best of each situation.
- rely on themselves to find something interesting in the class and learn the material.

Students with an external locus of control

- believe that their lives are largely a result of luck, fate, or chance.
- think that teachers give grades rather than students earn grades.
- rely on external motivation from teachers or others.
- look for someone to blame when they make a mistake.
- think negatively and believe they are victims of circumstance.
- rely on the teacher to make the class interesting and to teach the material.

Activity   Internal or External Locus of Control

Decide whether the statement represents an internal or external locus of control and put a checkmark in the appropriate column.

Internal	External	
_____	_____	1. Much of what happens to us is due to fate, chance, or luck.
_____	_____	2. Grades depend on how much work you put into it.
_____	_____	3. If I do badly on the test, it is usually because the teacher is unfair.
_____	_____	4. If I do badly on the test, it is because I didn't study or didn't understand the material.

_____	_____	5. I often get blamed for things that are not my fault.
_____	_____	6. I try to make the best of the situation.
_____	_____	7. It is impossible to get a good grade if you have a bad instructor.
_____	_____	8. I can be successful through hard work.
_____	_____	9. If the teacher is not there telling me what to do, I have a hard time doing my work.
_____	_____	10. I can motivate myself to study.
_____	_____	11. If the teacher is boring, I probably won't do well in class.
_____	_____	12. I can find something interesting about each class.
_____	_____	13. When bad things are going to happen, there is not much you can do about it.
_____	_____	14. I create my own destiny.
_____	_____	15. Teachers should motivate the students to study.
_____	_____	16. I have a lot of choice about what happens in my life.

As you probably noticed, the even-numbered statements represent internal locus of control. The odd-numbered statements represent external locus of control. Remember that students with an internal locus of control have a greater chance of success in college. It is important to see yourself as responsible for your own success and achievement and to believe that with effort you can achieve your goals.

> How can you use the concept of locus of control to improve your chances of success in college?

Affiliation

Human beings are social creatures who generally feel the need to be part of a group. This tendency is called affiliation motivation. People like to be part of a community, family, organization, or culture. You can apply this motivation technique in college by participating in student activities on campus. Join an athletic team, participate in a club, or join the student government. In this way you will feel like you are part of a group and will have a sense of belonging. College is more than going to class; it is participating in social activities, making new friends, and sharing new ideas. Twenty years after you graduate from college, you are more likely to remember the conversations held with college friends than the detailed content of classes. College provides the opportunity to become part of a new group and to start lifelong friendships.

Achievement

Some students are motivated by achievement. Individuals who are achievement motivated have a need for success in school, sports, careers, and other competitive situations. These individuals enjoy getting recognition for their success. They are often known as the best student, the outstanding athlete, or the employee of the year. These persons are attracted to careers that provide rewards for individual achievement, such as sales, law, architecture, engineering, and business. They work hard in order to enjoy the rewards of their efforts. In college, some students work very hard to achieve high grades and then take pride in their accomplishments. One disadvantage of using this type of motivation is that it can lead to excess stress. These students often need to remember to balance their time between work, school, family, and leisure so that they do not become too stressed by the need to achieve.

Applying the Principles of Learning

Psychologists believe that much of our behavior is learned. Understanding these principles of learning can give you some powerful tools for changing your own behavior. We frequently learn through a process called **operant conditioning**. A simple definition of operant conditioning is that behavior is increased or decreased depending on the consequences of the behavior. If you study for the test and receive an A, you will be more likely to study in the future. In operant conditioning, the consequences of a behavior lead to a change in the probability of its occurrence. We are always affected by the consequences of our behavior and are constantly in the process of learning.

If the consequences of your behavior are positive, you are positively reinforced as in our examples above. You are more likely to continue the behavior. If the consequences of your behavior are negative, that behavior is less likely to occur. For example, if you receive a traffic ticket and have to pay a large fine, you are less likely to repeat the offense.

You can use **positive reinforcement** on yourself to manage your own behavior. If you want to increase your studying behavior, follow it by a positive consequence or a reward. Think about what is rewarding to you (watching TV, playing sports, enjoying your favorite music). You could study (your behavior) and then watch a TV program (the positive reinforcement). The timing of your reward is important. To be effective, it must immediately follow the behavior. If you watch TV and then study, you may not get around to studying. If you watch the TV program tomorrow or next week, it is not a strong reinforcement because it is not an immediate reward.

Be careful about the kinds of rewards you use so that you do not get into habits that are detrimental to your health. If you use food as a reward for studying, you may increase your studying behavior, but you may also gain a few pounds. Using alcohol or drugs as a reward can start an addiction. Buying yourself a reward can ruin your budget. Good rewards do not involve too many calories, cost too much money, or involve alcohol or drugs.

You can also use a negative consequence to decrease a behavior. If you touch a hot stove and get burned, you quickly learn not to do it again. You could decide to miss your favorite television program if you do not complete your studying. However, this is not fun and you may feel deprived. You might even rebel and watch your favorite TV show anyway. See if you can find a way to use positive reinforcement (a reward) for increasing a behavior that is beneficial to you rather than using a negative consequence.

When we are young, our attitudes toward education are largely shaped by positive or negative reinforcement. If you were praised for being a good reader as a child, it is likely that you enjoyed reading and developed good reading skills. Maybe a teacher embarrassed you because of your math skills and you learned to be anxious about math. Think about areas of your education in which you excel, and see if you can recall someone praising or otherwise reinforcing that behavior. If you are a good athlete, did someone praise your athletic ability when you were younger? How was it rewarded? If you are not good at math, what were some early messages about your math performance? These early messages have a powerful influence on later behavior. You may need to put in some effort to learn new and more beneficial behaviors.

As a college student, you can use a reward as a powerful motivator. Praise yourself and think positively about your achievements in college even if the achievements come in small steps.

> What are some positive rewards that you can give yourself for studying? Remember, good rewards don't have too many calories, don't cost too much, and don't involve drugs or alcohol.

Success Is a Habit

We establish habits by taking small actions each day. Through repetition, these individual actions become habits. I once visited the Golden Gate Bridge in San Francisco and saw a cross section of the cable used to support the bridge. It was made of small metal strands twisted with other strands. Then the cables were twisted together to make a stronger cable. Habits are a lot like cables. We start with one small action and each successive action makes the habit stronger. Have you ever stopped to think that success can be a habit? We all have learned patterns of behavior that either help us to be successful or that interfere with our success. With some effort and some basic understanding of behavior modification, you can choose to establish some new behaviors that lead to success or to get rid of behaviors that interfere with it.

Seven Steps to Change a Habit

You can establish new habits that lead to your success. Once a habit is established, it can become a pattern of behavior that you do not need to think about very much. For example, new students often need to get into the habit of studying. Here is an outline of steps that can be helpful to establish new behaviors.

1. State the problem.
What are your roadblocks or obstacles? What new habit would you like to start? What bad habit would you like to change? Be truthful about it. This is sometimes the most difficult step.

2. Change one small behavior at a time.
If you think about climbing a mountain, the task can seem overwhelming. However, you can take the first step. If you can change one small behavior, you can gain the confidence to change another. For example, a goal to have a better diet is broad and vague. A good way to make it small is to say, "I plan to eat more fruits and vegetables each day." State the behavior you would like to change. Make it small.

3. State in a positive way the behavior you wish to establish.
For example, instead of the negative statement "I will not eat junk food," change it to "I plan to eat fruits and vegetables each day."

4. Count the behavior.
How often do you do this behavior? For example, if you are trying to stop smoking, it is helpful to count the number of cigarettes you smoke each day. If you are trying to improve your diet, write down everything that you eat each day. If you are trying to establish a pattern of studying, write down how much time you spend studying each day. Sometimes just getting an awareness of your habit is enough to begin to make some changes.

5. Picture in your mind the actions you might take.
For example: I see myself in the grocery store buying fruits and vegetables. I see myself packing these fruits and vegetables in my lunch. I see myself putting these foods in a place where I will notice them.

SEVEN STEPS TO CHANGE A HABIT

1. State the problem
2. Change one small behavior at a time
3. Be positive
4. Count the behavior
5. Picture the change
6. Practice the behavior
7. Reward yourself

6. Practice the behavior for ten days.

In ten days you can get started on a new pattern of behavior. Once you have started, keep practicing the behavior for about a month to firmly establish your new pattern of behavior. The first three days are the most difficult. If you fail, don't give up. Just realize that you are human and keep trying for ten days. Think positively that you can be successful. Write a journal or note on your calendar about what you have accomplished each day.

7. Find a reward for your behavior.

Remember that we tend to repeat behaviors that are positively reinforced. Find rewards that do not involve too many calories, don't cost too much money, and don't involve alcohol or drugs. Also, rewards are most effective if they directly follow the behavior you wish to reinforce.

Motivation

Test what you have learned by selecting the correct answer to the following questions:

1. If the behavior is followed by a reward,
   A. it is likely to be increased.
   B. it is likely to be decreased.
   C. there will probably be no effect.

2. For rewards to be effective, they must occur,
   A. before the behavior.
   B. immediately after the behavior.
   C. either before or after the behavior.

3. Manage your internal distractions by,
   A. forcing yourself to concentrate.
   B. telling yourself not to worry about your problems.
   C. noticing when your attention has wandered and choose where you want to focus your attention.

4. To be successful in college, it is best to use,
   A. intrinsic motivation.
   B. extrinsic motivation.
   C. external locus of control.

5. To change a habit,
   A. set high goals.
   B. focus on negative behavior.
   C. begin with a concrete behavior that can be counted.

How did you do on the quiz? Check your answers: 1. A, 2. B, 3. C, 4. A, 5. C

Persistence

There is an old saying that persistence will get you almost anything eventually. This saying applies to your success in college. The first two to six weeks of college are a critical time in which many students drop out. Realize that college is a new experience and that you will face new challenges and growth experiences. Make plans to persist, especially in the first few weeks. Get to know a college counselor or advisor. These professionals can help you to get started in the right classes and answer any questions you might have. It is important to make a connection with a counselor or faculty member so that you feel comfortable in college and have the resources to obtain needed help. Plan to enroll on time so that you do not have to register late. It is crucial to attend the first class. In the first class, the professor explains the class requirements and expectations and sets the tone for the class. You may even get dropped from the class if you are not there on the first day. Get into the habit of studying right away. Make studying a habit that you start immediately at the beginning of the semester or quarter. If you can make it through the first six weeks, it is likely that you can finish the semester and complete your college education.

It has been said that 90 percent of success is just showing up. Any faculty member will tell you that the number one reason for students dropping out of college is lack of attendance. They know that when students miss three classes in a row, they are not likely to return. Even very capable students who miss class may find that they are lost when they come back. Many students are simply afraid to return. Classes such as math and foreign languages are sequential, and it is very difficult to make up work after an absence. One of the most important ways you can be successful is to make a habit of consistently showing up for class.

You will also need commitment to be successful. Commitment is a promise to yourself to follow through with something. In athletics, it is not necessarily the one with the best physical skills that makes the best athlete. Commitment and practice make a great athlete. Commitment means doing whatever is necessary to succeed. Like the good athlete, make a commitment to accomplishing your goals. Spend the time necessary to be successful in your studies.

When you face difficulties, persistence and commitment are especially important. History is full of famous people who contributed to society through persistence and commitment. Consider these facts about Abraham Lincoln, for example.

- Failed in business at age 21.
- Was defeated in a legislative race at age 22.
- Failed again in business at age 24.
- Overcame the death of his sweetheart at age 26.
- Had a nervous breakdown at age 27.
- Lost a congressional race at age 34.
- Lost a congressional race at age 36.
- Lost a senatorial race at age 45.
- Failed in an effort to become Vice-President at age 47.
- Lost a senatorial race at age 49.
- Was elected President of the United States at age 52.[6]

You will face difficulties along the way in any worthwhile venture. The successful person keeps on trying. There are some precautions about persistence, however. Make sure that the goal you are trying to reach is attainable and valuable to you. As you learn more about yourself, you may want to change your goals. Also, persistence can be misguided if it involves other people. For example, if you decide that you want to marry someone and this someone does not want to marry you, it is better to focus your energy and attention on a different goal.

One of the best ways to be persistent is to accomplish your goals one step at a time. If you look at a mountain, it may seem too high to climb, but you can do it one step at a time. Araceli Segarra became the first Spanish woman to climb Mount Everest. At 29,028 feet, Mount Everest is the highest mountain in the world. It is so high that you need an oxygen tank to breathe at the top. So how did Araceli climb the mountain? She says that it took strength and concentration. She put one foot in front of the other. When she was near the top of the mountain, she was more tired than she had ever been in her life. She told herself that she would take ten more steps. When she took ten steps she said, "I'm OK. I made it." Then she took ten more steps until she reached the top of the mountain.

The goal of getting a college education may seem like a mountain that is difficult to climb. Break it into smaller steps that you can accomplish. See your college counselor or advisor, register for classes, attend the first class, read the first chapter, do the first assignment, and you will be on the road to your success. Then continue to break tasks into small, achievable steps and continue from one step to the next. And remember, persistence will get you almost anything eventually.

1. Are you generally persistent in reaching your goals?
2. Are there times when it's best to change goals rather than be persistent?

Success over the Internet

Visit the College Success website at www.cuyamaca.edu/collegesuccess/

The College Success website is continually updated with new topics and links to the material presented in this chapter. Topics include

- How to improve concentration
- Motivation
- Positive attitude
- Balancing work, school, and social life
- Success factors for new college students
- How to change a habit
- Dealing with cravings and urges

Contact your instructor if you have any problems accessing the College Success website.

Endnotes

1. U.S. Census Bureau, "The Big Payoff: Educational Attainment and Synthetic Estimates of Work-Life Earnings," July 2002, retrieved from http://www.census.gov
2. W. Lewallen, "The Impact of Being Undecided on College Persistence," *Journal of College Student Development 34* (1993): 103–12.
3. Marsha Fralick, "College Success: A Study of Positive and Negative Attrition," *Community College Review 20* (1993): 29–36.
4. Ideas from Lina Rocha, Personal Development Instructor, Cuyamaca College, El Cajon, CA.
5. M. J. Findlay and H. M. Cooper, "Locus of Control and Academic Achievement: A Literature Review," *Journal of Personality and Social Psychology 44* (1983): 419–27.
6. Anthony Robbins, *Unlimited Power* (New York: Ballantine Books, 1986), 73.

Managing Time and Money

Chapter 3

Chapter Focus

Read to answer these key questions:

What are my lifetime goals?   How can I manage my time to accomplish my goals?   How much time do I need for study and work?   How can I make an effective schedule?   What are some time management tricks?   How can I deal with procrastination?   How can I manage my money to accomplish my financial goals?   What are some ways to save money?   How can I pay for my education?   How can I use priorities to manage my time?

Success in college requires that you manage both time and money. You will need time to study and money to pay for your education. The first step in managing time and money is to think about the goals that you wish to accomplish in your life. Having goals that are important to you provides a reason and motivation for managing time and money. This chapter provides some useful techniques for managing time and money so that you can accomplish the goals you have set for yourself.

What Are My Lifetime Goals?

Setting goals helps you to establish what is important and provides direction for your life. Goals help you to focus your energy on what you want to accomplish. Goals are a promise to yourself to improve your life. Setting goals can help you turn your dreams into reality. Steven Scott in his book *A Millionaire's Notebook,* lays out five steps in this process:

1. Dream or visualize.
2. Convert the dream into goals.
3. Convert your goals into tasks.
4. Convert your task into steps.
5. Take your first step, and then the next.[1]

As you begin to think about your personal goals in life, make your goals specific and concrete. Rather than saying, "I want to be rich," make your goal something that you can break into specific steps. You might want to start learning about money management or begin a savings plan. Rather than setting a goal for happiness, think about what brings you happiness. If you want to live a long and healthy life, think about the health habits that will help you to accomplish your goal. You will need to break your goals down into specific tasks to be able to accomplish them.

From *College & Career Success*, 3rd edition by Marsha Fralick. Copyright © 2006 by Kendall/Hunt Publishing Company. Reprinted by permission.

> What are your lifetime goals? Begin your thinking about lifetime goals by answering the following questions:
>
> 1. What is your career goal? If you do not know what your career goal is, describe the work environment. Would your ideal career require a college degree? Would you work in an office or outside? Would you have the freedom to design your own projects or would you enjoy working in a more structured and stable environment? Would your career involve power and money? Would your career goal involve helping other people?
> 2. What are your family goals? Are you interested in marriage and family? What would be your important family values?
> 3. Describe your desired social life.
> 4. Where would you like to live, and what kind of house would you have?
> 5. What kind of recreational activities would you have?
> 6. When you are older and look back on your life, what are the three most important life goals that you would want to make sure to accomplish?

A Goal or a Fantasy?

One of the best questions ever asked in my class was, "What is the difference between a goal and a fantasy?" As you look at your list of lifetime goals, are some of these items goals or fantasies? Think about this question as you read the following scenario:

> *When Linda was a college student, she was walking through the parking lot and noticed a beautiful red sports car and decided that it would become a lifetime goal to own a similar car one day. However, with college expenses and her part-time job, it was not possible to buy the car. She would have to be content with the used car that her dad had given her so that she could drive to college. Years passed by, and Linda now has a good job, a home, and a family. She is reading a magazine and sees a picture of a similar red sports car. She cuts out this picture and tapes it to the refrigerator. After it has been on the refrigerator for several months, her children ask her why the picture is on the refrigerator. Linda replies, "I just like to dream about owning this car." One day as Linda is driving past a car dealership, she sees the red sports car on display and stops in for a test drive. To her surprise, she decides that she does not like driving the car. It doesn't fit her lifestyle either. She enjoys outdoor activities that would require a larger car. Buying a second car would be costly and reduce the amount of money that the family could spend on vacations. She decides that vacations are more important than owning the sports car. Linda goes home and removes the picture of the red sports car from the refrigerator.*

There are many differences between a goal and a fantasy. A fantasy is a dream that may or may not become a reality. A goal is something that we actually plan to achieve. Sometimes we begin with a fantasy and later it becomes a goal. A fantasy can become a goal if steps are taken to achieve it. In the preceding example, the sports car is a fantasy until Linda actually takes the car for a test drive. After driving the car, she decides that she really does not want it. The fantasy is sometimes better than the reality. Goals and fantasies change over a lifetime. We set goals, try them out, and change them as we grow and mature and find out what is most important in life. Knowing what we think is important, and what we value most, helps us make good decisions about lifetime goals.

What is the difference between a goal and a fantasy? A goal is something that requires action. Ask yourself if you are willing to take action on the goals you have set for yourself. Begin to take action by thinking about the steps needed to accomplish the goal. Then take the first step and continue. Change your goals if they are no longer important to you.

> Using one of the most important goals you have identified for yourself in the previous exercise, list some steps needed to accomplish it. What is the first step? Are you willing to begin taking these steps?

The ABCs of Time Management

The ABCs of time management is a system of thinking about priorities. Priorities are what you think is important. An **A priority** is a task that relates to your lifetime goal. For example, if my goal is to earn a college degree, studying becomes an A priority. This activity would become one of the most important tasks that I could accomplish today. If my goal were to be healthy, an A priority would be to exercise and plan a healthy diet. If my goal is to have a good family life, an A priority would be to spend time with family members. Knowing about your lifetime goals and spending time on those items that are most important to you will help you to accomplish the goals that you have set for yourself. If you do not spend time on your goals, you may want to look at them again and decide which ones are fantasies that you do not really value or want to accomplish.

A **B priority** is an activity that you have to do but is not directly related to your lifetime goal. Examples of B priorities might be getting out of bed, taking a shower, buying groceries, paying bills, or getting gas for the car. These activities are less important but still are necessary for survival. If I do not put gas in the car, I cannot even get to school or work. If I do not pay the bills, I will soon have financial difficulties. While we often cannot postpone these activities in order to accomplish lifetime goals, we can learn efficient time management techniques to accomplish these tasks quickly.

A **C priority** is something that I can postpone until tomorrow with no harmful effect. For example, I could wait until tomorrow or another day to wash my car, do the laundry, buy groceries, or organize my desk. As these items are postponed, however, they can move up the list to a B priority. If I cannot see out of my car window or have no clean clothes to wear, it is time to move these tasks up on my list of priorities.

Have you ever been a victim of "**C fever**"? This is an illness in which we do the C activities first and do not get around to doing the A activities that are connected to lifetime goals. Tasks required to accomplish lifetime goals are often ones that are more difficult, challenge our abilities and take some time to accomplish. These tasks are often more difficult than the B or C activities. The C activities can fill our time and exhaust the energy we need to accomplish the A activities. An example of C fever is the student who cleans the desk or organizes the CD collection instead of studying. C fever is doing the endless tasks that keep us from accomplishing goals that are really important to us. Why do we fall victim to C fever? C activities are often easy to do and give us a sense of accomplishment. We can see immediate progress without too much effort. I can wash my car and get a sense of accomplishment and satisfaction in my shiny clean car. The task is easy and does not challenge my intellectual capabilities.

Activity Setting Priorities

To see how the ABCs of time management work, read the profile of Justin, a typical college student, below.

Justin is a 19-year-old college student who plans to major in physical therapy. He is athletic and values his good health. He cares about people and likes helping others. He has a part-time job working as an assistant in the gym, where he monitors proper use of the weight-lifting machines. Justin is also a member of the soccer team and practices with the team every afternoon.

Here is a list of activities that Justin would like to do today. Label each task as follows:

    A if it relates to the Justin's lifetime goals
    B if it is something necessary to do
    C if it is something which could be done tomorrow or later

_____ Get up, shower, get dressed.
_____ Eat breakfast.
_____ Go to work.
_____ Go to class.
_____ Visit with friends between classes.
_____ Buy a new battery for his watch.
_____ Go shopping for new gym shoes.
_____ Attend soccer practice.
_____ Do weight-lifting exercises.

_____ Study for biology test that is tomorrow.
_____ Meet friends for pizza at lunch.
_____ Call girlfriend.
_____ Eat dinner.
_____ Unpack gear from weekend camping trip.
_____ Watch football game on TV.
_____ Play video games.
_____ Do math homework.

While Justin is the only one who can decide how to spend his time, he can take some steps toward accomplishing his lifetime goal of being healthy by eating properly, exercising, and going to soccer practice. He can become a physical therapist by studying for the biology test and doing his math homework. He can gain valuable experience related to physical therapy by working in the gym. He cares about people and likes to maintain good relationships with others. Any tasks related to these goals are high-priority A activities.

What other activities are necessary B activities? He certainly needs to get up, shower, and get dressed. What are the C activities that could be postponed until tomorrow or later? Again Justin needs to decide. Maybe he could postpone shopping for a new watch battery and gym shoes until the weekend. He would have to decide how much time to spend visiting with friends, watching TV, or playing video games. Since he likes these activities, he could use them as rewards for studying for the biology test and doing his math homework.

How to Estimate Study and Work Time

Students are often surprised at the amount of time necessary for study to be successful in college. A general rule is that you need to study two hours for every hour spent in a college class. A typical weekly schedule of a full-time student would look like this:

Typical College Schedule

    15 hours of attending class
    +30 hours of reading, studying, and preparation
    45 hours total

A full-time job involves working 40 hours a week. A full-time college student spends 45 hours or more attending classes and studying. Some students will need more than 45 hours a week if they are taking lab classes, need help with study and learning skills, or are taking a heavy course load.

Some students try to work full-time and go to school full-time. While some are successful, this schedule is extremely difficult.

The Nearly Impossible Schedule

```
 15 hours attending class
 30 hours studying
+40 hours working
 85 hours total
```

This schedule is the equivalent of having two full-time jobs! Working full-time makes it very difficult to find the time necessary to study for classes. Lack of study causes students to do poorly on exams and to doubt their abilities. Such a schedule causes stress and fatigue that make studying difficult. Increased stress can also lead to problems with personal relationships and emotional problems. These are all things that lead to dropping out of college.

Many students today work and go to college. Working during college can provide some valuable experience that will help you to find a job when you finish college. Working can teach you to manage your time efficiently and give you a feeling of independence and control over your own future. Many people need to work to pay for their education. A general guideline is to work no more than 20 hours a week if you plan to attend college full-time. Here is a workable schedule.

Part-Time Work Schedule

```
 12 hours attending class
 24 hours studying
+20 hours working
 56 hours total
```

A commitment of 56 hours a week is like having a full-time job and a part-time job. While this schedule takes extra energy and commitment, many students are successful with it. Notice that the course load is reduced to 12 hours. This schedule involves taking one less class per semester. The class missed can be made up in summer school, or the time needed to graduate can be extended. Many students take five years to earn the bachelor's degree because they work part-time. It is better to take longer to graduate than to drop out of college or to give up because of frustration. If you must work full-time, consider reducing your course load to one or two courses. You will gradually reach your goal of a college degree.

Part-Time Student Schedule

```
  6 hours attending class
 12 hours studying
+40 hours working
 58 hours total
```

Add up the number of hours you are attending classes, double this figure for study time and add to it your work time as in the above examples. How many hours of commitment do you have? Can you be successful with your current level of commitment to school, work, and study?

To begin managing your schedule, use the weekly calendar located at the end of this chapter to write in your scheduled activities such as work, class times, and athletics.

Schedule Your Success

If you have not used a schedule in the past, consider trying a schedule for a couple of weeks to see if it is helpful in completing tasks and working toward your lifetime goals. There are several advantages to using a schedule:

- It gets you started on your work.
- It helps you avoid procrastination.
- It relieves pressure because you have things under control.
- It frees the mind of details.
- It helps you find time to study.
- It eliminates the panic caused by doing things at the last minute.
- It helps you find time for recreation and exercise.

Once you have made a master schedule that includes classes, work, and other activities, you will see that you have some blanks that provide opportunities for using your time productively. Here are some ideas for making the most of your schedule:

1. Fill in your study times. Use the time immediately before class for previewing and the time immediately after class for reviewing. Remember that you need to study two hours or more for each hour spent in a college class.
2. Break large projects such as a term paper or test into small tasks and begin early. Double your time estimates for completion of the project. Larger projects often take longer than you think. If you finish early, use the extra time for something fun.
3. Use the daylight hours when you are most alert for studying. It may take you longer to study if you wait until late in the day when you're tired.
4. Think about your day and see if you can determine when you are most alert and awake. Prime time differs with individuals, but it is generally earlier in the day. Use the prime time when you are most alert to accomplish your most challenging tasks. For example, do your math homework during prime time. Wash your clothes during nonprime time, when you are likely to be less alert.
5. Set priorities. Make sure you include activities related to your lifetime goals.
6. Allow time for sleep and meals. It is easier to study if you are well rested and have good eating habits.
7. Schedule your time in manageable blocks of an hour or two. Having every moment scheduled leads to frustration when plans change.
8. Leave some time unscheduled to use as a shock absorber. You will need unscheduled time to relax and to deal with unexpected events.
9. Leave time for recreation, exercise, and fun.

Return to the schedule at the end of this chapter. After you have written in classes, work times, and other scheduled activities, use the scheduling ideas listed earlier to write in your study times and other activities related to your lifetime goals. Leave some unscheduled time to provide flexibility in the schedule.

If You Dislike Schedules

Some personality types like more freedom and do not like the structure that a schedule provides. There are alternatives for those who do not like to use a schedule. Here are some additional ideas.

1. A simple and fast way to organize your time is to use a to-do list. Take an index card or small piece of paper and simply write a list of what you need to do during the day.

You can prioritize the list by putting an A or star by the most important items. Cross items off the list as you accomplish them. A list helps you focus on what is important and serves as a reminder not to forget certain tasks.

2. Another idea is to use monthly or yearly calendars to write down important events, tasks, and deadlines. Use these calendars to note the first day of school, when important assignments are due, vacations, and final exams. Place the calendars in a place where they are easily seen.
3. Alan Lakein, who wrote a book titled *How to Get Control of Your Time and Your Life,* suggests a simple question to keep you on track.[2] Lakein's question is, "What is the best use of my time right now?" This question works well if you keep in mind your goals and priorities.
4. Use reminders and sticky notes to keep on track and to remind yourself of what needs to be done each day. Place the notes in a place where you will see them, such as your computer, the bathroom mirror, or the dashboard of your car.
5. Some families use their refrigerator as a time management device. Use the refrigerator to post your calendars, reminders, goals, tasks and to-do lists. You will see these reminders every time you open the refrigerator.
6. Invent your own unique ideas for managing time. Anything will work if it helps to accomplish your goals.

Time Management, Part I

Test what you have learned by selecting the correct answer to the following questions.

1. The most important difference between a goal and a fantasy is
    A. imagination.
    B. procrastination.
    C. action.
2. An A priority is
    A. related to your lifetime goals.
    B. something important.
    C. something you have to do.
3. A general rule for college success is that you must spend _____ hours studying for every hour spent in a college class.
    A. one hour
    B. four hours
    C. two hours
4. For a workable study schedule,
    A. fill in all the blank time slots.
    B. leave some unscheduled time to deal with the unexpected.
    C. plan to study late at night.
5. To complete a large project such as a term paper,
    A. break the project into small tasks and begin early.
    B. schedule large blocks of time the day before the paper is due.
    C. leave time for exercise, recreation, and fun before beginning on the project.

How did you do on the quiz? Check your answers: 1. C, 2. A, 3. C, 4. B, 5. A

> List ten items that you have to do today. Place an A next to the items that are related to your lifetime goals.

Time Management Tricks

Life is full of demands for work, study, family, friends, and recreation. Time management tricks can help you get started on the important tasks and make the most of your time. Try the following techniques when you are feeling frustrated and overwhelmed.

Divide and Conquer

When large tasks seem overwhelming, think of the small tasks needed to complete the project and start on the first step. For example, suppose you have to write a term paper. You have to take out a paper and pencil, log onto your computer, brainstorm some ideas, go to the library to find information, think about your main ideas, and write the first sentence. Each of these steps is manageable. It's looking at the entire project that can be intimidating.

I once set out hiking on a mountain trail. When I got to the top of the mountain and looked down, I enjoyed a spectacular view and was amazed at how high I had climbed. If I had thought about how high the mountain was, I might not have attempted the hike. I climbed the mountain by taking it one step at a time. That's the secret to completing any large project. Break it into small, manageable parts; then take the first step and keep going.

Learning a small part at a time is also easy and helps with motivation for learning. While in college, carry around some material that you need to study. Take advantage of five or ten minutes of time to study a small part of your material. In this way you make good use of your time and enhance memory by using distributed practice. Don't wait until you have large blocks of uninterrupted study time to begin your studies. You may not have the luxury of large blocks of time, or you may want to spend that time in other ways.

Do the First Small Step

The most difficult step in completing any project is the first step. If you have a challenging project to do, think of a small first step and complete that small step. Make the first step something that you can accomplish easily and in a short amount of time. Give yourself permission to stop after the first step. However, you may find that you are motivated to continue with the project. If you have a term paper to write, think about some small step you can take to get started. Log onto your computer and look at the blank screen. Start writing some ideas. Type the topic into a computer search engine and see what information is available. Go to the library and see what is available on your topic. If you can find some interesting ideas, you can motivate yourself to begin the project. Once you have started the project, it is easier to continue.

The 80/20 Rule

Alan Lakein is noted for many useful time management techniques. One that I have used over the years is the 80/20 rule. Lakein says, "If all items are arranged in order of value, 80 percent of the value would come from only 20 percent of the items, while the remaining 20 percent of the value would come from 80 percent of the items."[3] For example, if you have a list of ten items to do, two of the items on the list are more important than the others. If you were to do only the two most important items, you would have accomplished 80 percent of the value. If you are short on time, see if you can choose the 20 percent of the tasks that are the most valuable. Lakein noted that the 80/20 rule applies to many situations in life:

TIME MANAGEMENT TRICKS

–Divide and conquer
–First small steps
–80/20 rule
–Aim for excellence, not perfection
–Make learning fun
–Take a break
–Study in the library
–Say no

- 80 percent of file usage is in 20 percent of the files.
- 80 percent of dinners repeat 20 percent of the recipes.
- 80 percent of the washing is done on the 20 percent of the clothes worn most frequently.
- 80 percent of the dirt is on 20 percent of the floor used most often.

Think about how the 80/20 rule applies in your life. I know that I wear 20 percent of my clothes 80 percent of the time. I also know that I use 20 percent of my files 80 percent of the time. The 80/20 rule is another way of thinking about priorities and figuring out which of the tasks are C priorities. This prioritizing is especially important if you are short on time. The 80/20 rule helps you to focus on what is most important.

Aim for Excellence, Not Perfection

Are you satisfied with your work only if it is done perfectly? Do you put off a project because you cannot do it perfectly? Aiming for perfection in all tasks causes anxiety and procrastination. There are times when perfection is necessary. Dave Ellis calls this time management technique "It Ain't No Piano."[4] If a construction worker bends a nail in the framing of a house, it does not matter. The construction worker simply puts in another nail. After all, "it ain't no piano." It is another matter if you are building a fine cabinet or finishing a piano. Perfection is more important in these circumstances. We need to ask: Is the task important enough to invest the time needed for perfection? A final term paper needs to be as perfect as we can make it. A rough draft is like the frame of a house that does not need to be perfect.

In aiming for excellence rather than perfection, challenge yourself to use perspective to see the big picture. How important is the project and how perfect does it need to be? Could your time be better invested accomplishing other tasks? This technique requires flexibility and the ability to change with different situations. Do not give up if you cannot complete a project perfectly. Do the best that you can in the time available. In some situations, if life is too hectic, you may need to settle for completing the project and getting it in on time rather than doing it perfectly. With this idea in mind, you may be able to relax and still achieve excellence.

Make Learning Fun by Finding a Reward

Time management is not about restriction, self-control, and deprivation. Used correctly, time can be used to get more out of life and to have fun while doing it. Remember that behavior is likely to increase if followed by a reward. Think about activities that you find rewarding. In our time management example with Justin who wants to be a physical therapist, he could use many tasks as rewards for completing his studies. He could meet friends for pizza, call his girlfriend, play video games, or watch TV. The key idea is to do the studying first and then reward the behavior. Maybe Justin will not be able to do all of the activities we have mentioned as possible rewards, but he could choose what he enjoys most.

Studying first and then rewarding yourself leads to peace of mind and the ability to focus on tasks at hand. While Justin is out having pizza with his friends, he does not have to worry about work that he has not done. While Justin is studying, he does not have to feel that he is being deprived of having pizza with friends. In this way, he can focus on studying while he is studying and focus on having a good time while relaxing with his friends. It is not a good idea to think about having pizza with friends while studying or to think about studying while having pizza with friends. When you work, focus on your work and get it done. When you play, enjoy playing without having to think about work.

Take a Break

"Don't say you don't have enough time. You have exactly the same number of hours per day that were given to Helen Keller, Pasteur, Michelangelo, Mother Theresa, Leonardo da Vinci, Thomas Jefferson, and Albert Einstein."
H. JACKSON BROWN

If you are overwhelmed with the task at hand, sometimes it is best to just take a break. If you're stuck on a computer program or a math problem, take a break and do something else. As a general rule, take a break of ten minutes for each hour of study. During the break, do something totally different. It is a good idea to get up and move around. Get up and pet your cat or dog, observe your goldfish, or shoot a few baskets. If time is really a premium, use your break time to accomplish other important tasks. Put your clothes in the dryer, empty the dishwasher, or pay a bill.

Study in the Library

If you are having difficulty with studying, try studying at school in the library. Libraries are designed for studying, and other people are studying there as well. It is hard to do something else in the library without annoying the librarian or other students. If you can complete your studying at school, you can go home and relax. This may be especially important if family, friends, or roommates at home easily distract you.

Learn to Say No Sometimes

Learn to say no to tasks that you do not have time to do. Follow your statement with the reasons for saying no: you are going to college and need time to study. Most people will understand this answer and respect it. You may need to say no to yourself as well. Maybe you cannot go out on Wednesday night if you have a class early on Thursday morning. Maybe the best use of your time right now is to turn off the TV or get off the Internet and study for tomorrow's test. You are investing your time in your future.

> What time management techniques can you use to accomplish your goal of getting a college degree?

Dealing with Time Bandits

Time bandits are the many things that keep us from spending time on the things we think are important. Another word for a time bandit is a time waster. In college, it is tempting to do many things other than studying. We are all victims of different kinds of bandits.

Activity

Put a checkmark next to the items that waste your time. Add your own personal time wasters at the end of the list.

____ TV	____ Other electronic devices	____ Daydreaming
____ Stereo	____ Saying yes when you mean no	____ Friends
____ Internet	____ Social time	____ Family
____ Phone	____ Household chores	____ Roommates
____ Video games	____ Partying	____ Children
____ CD player	____ Waiting time	____ Girlfriend, boyfriend, spouse

____ Sleeping in   ____ Shopping   ____ Being easily distracted
____ Studying at a bad time   ____ Reading magazines   ____ Studying in a distracting
____ Movies   ____ Commuting time (travel)   place

List some of your personal time bandits here.

_____

_____

Here are some ideas for keeping time bandits under control:

Schedule time for other people. Friends and family are important, so we do not want to get rid of them! Discuss your goal of a college education with your friends and family. People who care about you will respect your goals. You may need to use a Do Not Disturb sign at times. If you are a parent, remember that you are a role model for your children. If they see you studying, they are more likely to value their own education. Plan to spend quality time with your children and the people who are important to you. Make sure they understand that you care about them.

Remember the rewards. Many of the time bandits listed above make good rewards for completing your work. Put the time bandits to work for you by studying first and then enjoying a reward. Enjoy the TV, Internet, CD player, video games, or phone conversations after you have finished your studies. Aim for a balance of work, study, and leisure time.

Use your prime time wisely. Prime time is when you are most awake and alert. Use this time for studying. Use non-prime time for the time bandits. When you are tired, do household chores and shopping. If you have little time for household chores, you might find faster ways to do them. If you don't have time for shopping, you will notice that you spend less and have a better chance of following your budget.

Remind yourself about your priorities. When time bandits attack, remind yourself of why you are in college. Think about your personal goals for the future. Remember that college is not forever. By doing well in college, you will finish in the shortest time possible.

Use a schedule. Using a schedule or a to-do list is helpful in keeping you on track. Make sure you have some slack time in your schedule to handle unexpected phone calls and deal with the unplanned events that happen in life. If you cannot stick to your schedule, just get back on track as soon as you can.

> What are some of your personal time bandits? How can you manage your time bandits to make sure you have time to accomplish your important goals?

Dealing with Procrastination

Procrastination means putting off things until later. We all use delaying tactics at times. Procrastination that is habitual, however, can be self-destructive. Understanding some possible reasons for procrastination can help you use time more effectively and be more successful in accomplishing goals.

Why Do We Procrastinate?

There are many psychological reasons for procrastinating. Just becoming aware of these may help you deal with procrastination. If you have serious difficulty managing your time for psychological reasons, visit the counseling center at your college or university. Do you recognize any of these reasons for procrastination in yourself or others?

Fear of failure. Sometimes we procrastinate because we are afraid of failing. We see our performance as related to how much ability we have and how worthwhile we are as human beings. We may procrastinate in our college studies because of doubts about our ability to do the work. Success, however, comes from trying and learning from mistakes. There is a popular saying: falling down is not failure, but failing to get up or not even trying is failure.

Fear of success. Most students are surprised when I say that one of the reasons for procrastination is fear of success. Success in college means moving on with your life, getting a job, leaving a familiar situation, accepting increased responsibility, and sometimes leaving friends behind. None of these tasks is easy. An example of fear of success is not taking the last step required to be successful. Students sometimes do not take the last class needed to graduate. Some good students do not show up for the final exam or do not turn in a major project. If you ever find yourself procrastinating on an important last step, ask yourself if you are afraid of success and what lies ahead in your future.

Perfectionism. Some people who procrastinate do not realize that they are perfectionists. Perfectionists expect more from themselves than is realistic and more than others expect of themselves. There is often no other choice than to procrastinate because perfectionism is usually unattainable. Perfectionism generates anxiety that further hinders performance. Perfectionists need to understand that perfection is seldom possible. They need to set a time limit on projects and do their best within those time limits.

Need for excitement. Some students can only be motivated by waiting until the last minute to begin a project. These students are excited and motivated by playing a game of "Beat the Clock." They like living on the edge and the adrenaline rush of responding to a crisis. Playing this game provides motivation, but it does not leave enough time to achieve the best results. Inevitably, things happen at the last minute to make the game even more exciting and dangerous: the printer breaks, the computer crashes, the student gets ill, the car breaks down, or the dog eats the homework. These students need to start projects earlier to improve their chances of success. It is best to seek excitement elsewhere, in sports or other competitive activities.

Excellence without effort. In this scenario, students believe that they are truly outstanding and can achieve success without effort. These students think that they can go to college without attending classes or reading the text. They believe that they can pass the test without studying. They often do not succeed in college the first semester, which puts them at risk of dropping out of school. They often return to college later and improve their performance by putting in the effort required.

Loss of control. Some students fear loss of control over their lives and procrastinate to gain control. An example is students who attend college because others (such as parents) want them to attend. Procrastination becomes a way of gaining control over the situation by saying, "You can't make me do this." They attend college but accomplish nothing. Parents can support and encourage education, but students need to choose their own goals in life and attend college because it is important to them.

Tips for Dealing with Procrastination

When you find yourself procrastinating on a certain task, think about the consequences. Will the procrastination lead to failing an exam or getting a low grade? Think about the rewards of doing the task. If you do well, you can take pride in yourself and celebrate your success. How will you feel when the task is completed? Will you be able to enjoy your leisure time without guilt about not doing your work? How does the task help you to achieve your lifetime goals?

Maybe the procrastination is a warning sign that you need to reconsider lifetime goals and change them to better suit your needs.

PROCRASTINATION SCENARIO

George is a college student who is on academic probation for having low grades. He is required to make a plan for improving grades in order to remain in college. George tells the counselor that he is making poor grades because of his procrastination. He is an accounting major and puts off doing homework because he dislikes it and does not find it interesting. The counselor asks George why he had chosen accounting as a major. He replies that accounting is a major that is in demand and has a good salary. The counselor suggests that George consider a major that he would enjoy more. After some consideration, George changes his major to psychology. He becomes more interested in college studies and is able to raise his grades to stay in college.

Most of the time, you will reap benefits by avoiding procrastination and completing the task at hand. Jane Burka and Lenora Yuen suggest the following steps to deal with procrastination:

1. Select a goal.
2. Visualize your progress.
3. Be careful not to sabotage yourself.
4. Stick to a time limit.
5. Don't wait until you feel like it.
6. Follow through. Watch out for excuses and focus on one step at a time.
7. Reward yourself after you have made some progress.
8. Be flexible about your goal.
9. Remember that it does not have to be perfect.[5]

Time Management, Part II

Test what you have learned by selecting the correct answer to the following questions.

1. To get started on a challenging project,
    A. think of a small first step and complete it.
    B. wait until you have plenty of time to begin.
    C. wait until you are well-rested and relaxed.
2. In completing a To Do List of 10 items, the 80/20 rule states that
    A. 80% of the value comes from completing most of the items on the list.
    B. 80% of the value comes from completing two of the most important items.
    C. 80% of the value comes from completing half of the items on the list.

3. It is suggested that students aim for
   A. perfection.
   B. excellence.
   C. passing.

4. Sometimes students procrastinate because of
   A. fear of failure.
   B. fear of success.
   C. all of the above.

5. Playing the game "Beat the Clock" when doing a term paper results in
   A. increased motivation and success.
   B. greater excitement and quality work.
   C. increased motivation and risk.

How did you do on the quiz? Check your answers: 1. A, 2. B, 3. B, 4. C, 5. C

What techniques can you use to avoid procrastination in accomplishing the goals that are important to you?

Managing Your Money

To be successful in college and in life, you will need to manage not only time but money. One of the top reasons that students drop out of college is that they cannot pay for their education or that they have to work so much that they do not have time for school. Take a look at your lifetime goals. Most students have a goal related to money, such as becoming financially secure or becoming wealthy. If financial security or wealth is one of your goals, you will need to begin to take some action to accomplish that goal. If you don't take action on a goal, it is merely a fantasy.

How to Become a Millionaire

Save regularly. Frances Leonard, author of *Time Is Money,* cites some statistics on how much money you need to save to become a millionaire.[6] You can retire with a million dollars by age 68 by saving the following amounts of money at various ages. These figures assume a 10 percent return on your investment.

At age 22, save $87 per month
At age 26, save $130 per month
At age 30, save $194 per month
At age 35, save $324 a month

Notice that the younger you start saving, the less money is required to reach the million-dollar goal. (And keep in mind that even a million dollars may not be enough money to save for retirement.) How can you start saving money when you are a student struggling to pay for college? The answer is to practice money management techniques and to begin a savings habit, even if the money you save is a small amount to buy your books for next semester. When you get that first good job, save 10 percent of the money. If you are serious about becoming financially secure, learn about investments such as real estate, stocks and bonds, and mutual funds. Learning how to save and invest your money can pay big dividends in the future.

Think thrifty. Money management begins with looking at your attitude toward money. Pay attention to how you spend your money so that you can accomplish your financial goals such as getting a college education, buying a house or car, or saving for the future. The following example shows how one woman accomplished her financial goals through being thrifty. Amy Dacyczyn, author of *The Tightwad Gazette* says, "A lot of people get a thrill out of buying things. Frugal people get a rush from the very act of saving. Saving can actually be fun—we think of it almost as a sport."[7] She noticed that people are working harder and harder for less and less. Amy Dacyczyn had the goals of marriage, children, and a New England farmhouse to live in. She wanted to stay home and take care of her six children instead of working. In seven years she was able to accomplish her goals with her husband's income of $30,000 a year. During this time she saved $49,000 for the down payment on a rural farmhouse costing $125,000. She also paid cash for $38,000 worth of car, appliance, and furniture purchases while staying at home with her children. How did she do this? She says that she just started paying attention to how she was spending her money.

To save money, Amy Dacyczyn made breakfast from scratch. She made oatmeal, pancakes, and muffins instead of purchasing breakfast cereals. She saved $440 a year in this way. She purchased the family clothing at yard sales. She thought of so many ideas to save money that she began publishing *The Tightwad Gazette* to share her money saving ideas with others. At $12 per subscription, she grosses a million dollars a year!

Challenge yourself to pay attention to how you spend your money and make a goal of being thrifty in order to accomplish your financial goals. With good money management, you can work less and have more time for college and recreational activities.

MANAGING YOUR MONEY
–Monitor your spending
–Prepare a budget
–Beware of credit and interest
–Watch spending leaks

Budgeting: The Key to Money Management

It is important to control your money, rather than letting your money control you. One of the most important things that you can do to manage your money and begin saving is to use a budget. A budget helps you become aware of how you spend your money and will help you make a plan for how you would like to spend your money.

Monitor how you spend your money. The first step in establishing a workable budget is to monitor how you are actually spending your money at the present time. For one month, keep a list of the date, purchase, and amount of money spent. You can do this on a sheet of paper, on your calendar, or on index cards. If you write checks for items, include the checks written as part of your money monitor. At the end of the month, group your purchases in categories such as food, gas, entertainment, and credit card payments and add them up. Doing this will yield some surprising results. For example, you may not be aware of just how much it costs to eat at a fast-food restaurant or to buy lunch or coffee every day.

Prepare a budget. One of the best tools for managing your money is a budget. At the end of this chapter you will find a simple budget sheet that you can use as a college student. After you finish college, update your budget and continue to use it. Follow these three steps to make a budget:

1. Write down your income for the month.
2. List your expenses. Include tuition, books, supplies, rent, telephone, utilities (gas, electric, water, cable TV), car payments, car insurance, car maintenance (oil, repairs), parking fees, food, personal grooming, clothes, entertainment, savings, credit card payments, loan payments, and other bills. Use your money monitor to discover how you are spending your money and include categories that are unique to you.
3. Subtract your total expenses from your total income. You cannot spend more than you have. Make adjustments as needed.

"Money is, in some respects like fire; it is a very excellent servant, but a terrible master."
P. T. BARNUM

Beware of credit and interest. College students are often tempted to use credit cards to pay for college expenses. This type of borrowing is costly and difficult to repay. It is easy to pull out a plastic credit card and buy items that you need and want. Credit card companies earn a great deal of money from credit cards. Jane Bryant Quinn gives an example of the cost of credit cards.[8] She says that if you owe $3,000 at 18 percent interest and pay the minimum payment of $60 per month, it will take you thirty years and ten months to get out of debt! Borrowing the $3,000 would cost about $22,320 over this time! If you use a credit card, make sure you can pay it off in one to three months. It is good to have a credit card in order to establish credit and to use in an emergency.

Watch those spending leaks. We all have spending problem areas. Often we spend small amounts of money each day that add up to large spending leaks over time. For example, if you spend $2 on coffee each weekday for a year, this adds up to $520 a year! If you eat lunch out each weekday and spend $6 for lunch, this adds up to $1,560 a year. Here are some common areas for spending leaks:

- Fast food and restaurants
- Entertainment and vacations
- Clothing
- Miscellaneous cash
- Gifts

To identify your spending problem areas, write down all of your expenditures for one month. Place a three-by-five card in your wallet to monitor your cash expenditures. At the end of the month, organize your expenditures into categories and total them up. Then ask yourself if this is how you want to spend your money.

Need More Money?

You may be tempted to work more hours to balance your budget. Remember that to be a full-time college student, it is recommended that you work no more than 20 hours per week. If you work more than 20 hours per week, you will probably need to decrease your course load. Before increasing your work hours, see if there is a way you can decrease your monthly expenses. Can you make your lunch instead of eating out? Can you get by without a car? Is the item you are purchasing a necessity, or do you just want to have it? These choices are yours.

Check out financial aid. All students can qualify for some type of financial aid. Visit the Financial Aid Office at your college for assistance. Depending on your income level, you may qualify for one or more of the following forms of aid.

Loans. A loan must be paid back. The interest rate and terms vary according to your financial need. With some loans, the federal government pays the interest while you are in school.

Grants. A grant does not need to be repaid. There are both state and federal grants based on need.

Work/Study. You may qualify for a federally subsidized job depending on your financial need.

The first step in applying for financial aid is to fill out the Free Application for Federal Student Aid (FAFSA). This form determines your eligibility for financial aid. You can obtain this form from your college's financial aid office or over the Internet at

www.fafsa.ed.gov/

Here are some other financial aid resources that you can obtain from your financial aid office or over the Internet.

Student Guide. The Student Guide, published by the U.S. Department of Education, describes in detail the kinds of financial aid available and eligibility requirements. It is available over the Internet at

studentaid.ed.gov/students/publications/student_guide/index.html

How to Apply for Financial Aid. Learn how to apply for federal financial aid and scholarships at this website

www.finaid.org/

The Student Guideline. Find out ways to fund your education, including tax cuts for education, loans, and other sources of financial aid at

www.ed.gov/offices/OSFAP/Students/student.html

Apply for a scholarship. Applying for a scholarship is like having a part-time job, only the pay is often better, the hours are flexible, and you can be your own boss. For this part-time job, you will need to research scholarship opportunities and fill out applications. There are multitudes of scholarships available, and sometimes no one even applies for them. Some students do not apply for scholarships because they think that high grades and financial need are required. While many scholarships are based on grades and financial need, many are not. Any person or organization can offer a scholarship for any reason they want. For example, scholarships can be based on hobbies, parent's occupation, religious background, military service, and personal interests, to name a few.

There are several ways to research a scholarship. As a first step, visit the financial aid office on your college campus. This office is staffed with persons knowledgeable about researching and applying for scholarships. Organizations or persons wishing to fund scholarships often contact this office to advertise opportunities.

You can also research scholarships through your public or college library. Ask the reference librarian for assistance. You can use the Internet to research scholarships as well. Use a search engine such as yahoo.com and simply type in the keyword *scholarships*. The following websites index thousands of scholarships:

fastweb.com
princetonreview.com/college/finance
college-scholarships.com/
guaranteed-scholarships.com/
collegenet.com/mach25/
srnexpress.com/index.cfm
collegeboard.com/paying
collegeanswer.com/index.jsp

To apply for scholarships, start a file of useful material usually included in scholarship applications. You can use this same information to apply for many scholarships.

- Three current letters of recommendation
- A statement of your personal goals
- A statement of your financial need
- Copies of your transcripts
- Copies of any scholarship applications you have filled out

Be aware of scholarship scams. You do not need to pay money to apply for a scholarship. No one can guarantee that you will receive a scholarship. Use your college scholarship office and your own resources to research and apply for scholarships.

The Best Ideas for Becoming Financially Secure

Financial planners provide the following ideas as the best way to build wealth and independence.[9] If you have financial security as your goal, plan to do the following.

1. *Use a simple budget to track income and expenses.* Do not spend more than you earn.
2. *Have a financial plan.* Include goals such as saving for retirement, purchasing a home, paying for college or taking vacations.
3. *Save 10 percent of your income.* As a college student, you may not be able to save this much, but plan to do it as soon as you get your first good-paying job. If you cannot save 10 percent, save something to get in the habit of saving. Save to pay for your tuition and books.
4. *Don't take on too much debt.* Be especially careful about credit cards and consumer debt. Credit card companies often visit college campuses and offer high-interest credit cards to students. It is important to have a credit card, but pay off the balance each month. Consider student loans instead of paying college fees by credit card.
5. *Don't procrastinate.* The earlier you take these steps toward financial security, the better.

Tips for Managing Your Money

Keeping these guidelines in mind can help you to manage your money.

- Don't let friends pressure you into spending too much money. If you can't afford something, learn to say no.
- Keep your checking account balanced or use online banking so you will know how much money you have.
- Don't lend money to friends. If your friends cannot manage their money, your loan will not help them.
- Use comparison shopping to find the best prices on the products that you buy.
- Get a part-time job while in college. You will earn money and gain valuable job experience.
- Don't use shopping as a recreational activity. When you visit the mall, you will find things you never knew you needed and will wind up spending more money than intended.
- Make a budget and follow it. This is the best way to achieve your financial goals.

> What is your plan for managing your money?

Do What Is Important First

The most important thing you can do to manage time and money is to spend it on what is most important. Manage time and money to help you live the life you want. How can you do this? Author Steven Covey wrote a book titled *The Seven Habits of Highly Effective People*. One of the habits is "Put first things first." Covey suggests that in time management, the "challenge is not to manage our time but to manage ourselves."[10]

How can you manage yourself? Our first thoughts in answering this question often involve suggestions about willpower, restriction, and self-control. Schedules and budgets are seen as instruments for self-control. It seems that the human spirit resists attempts at control, even when we aim to control ourselves. Often the response to control is rebellion. With time and money management, we may not follow a schedule or budget. A better approach to begin managing yourself is to know your values. What is important in your life? Do you have a clear mental picture of what is important? Can you describe your values and make a list of what is important to you? With your values and goals in mind, you can begin to manage both your time and your money.

When you have given some thought to your values, you can begin to set goals. When you have established goals for your life, you can begin to think in terms of what is most important and establish your priorities. Knowing your values is essential in making decisions about how to invest your time and money. Schedules and budgets are merely tools for helping you accomplish what you have decided is important. Time and money management is not about restriction and control but about making decisions regarding what is important in your life. If you know what is important, you can find the strength to say no to activities and expenditures that are less important.

As a counselor, I have the pleasure of working with many students who have recently explored and discovered their values and are highly motivated to succeed. They are willing to do what is important first. I recently worked with a young couple who came to enroll in college. They brought with them their young baby. The new father was interested in environmental engineering. He told me that in high school he never saw a reason for school and did just the minimum needed to get by. He was working as a construction laborer and making a living but did not see a future in the occupation. He had observed an environmental engineer who worked for the company and decided that was what he wanted for his future. As he looked at his new son, he told me that he needed to have a better future for himself and his family.

He and his wife decided to do what was important first. They were willing to make the sacrifice to attend school and invest the time needed to be successful. The father planned to work during the day and go to school at night. Later, he would go to school full-time and get a part-time job in the evening. His wife was willing to get a part-time job also, and they would share in taking care of the baby. They were willing to manage their money carefully to accomplish their goals. As they left, they added that their son would be going to college as well.

How do you get the energy to work all day, go to school at night, and raise a family? You can't do it by practicing self-control. You find the energy by having a clear idea of what you want in your life and focusing your time and resources on the goal. Finding what you want to do with your life is not easy either. Many times people find what they want to do when some significant event happens in their lives.

Begin to think about what you want out of life. Make a list of your important values and write down your lifetime goals. Don't forget about the people who are important to you and include them in your priorities. Then you will be able to do what is important first.

Success over the Internet

Visit the College Success website at www.cuyamaca.edu/collegesuccess/

The College Success website is continually updated with new topics and links to the material presented in this chapter. Topics include

- ▲ Suggestions for time management
- ▲ How to overcome procrastination

- How to deal with perfectionism
- Goal setting
- Goal setting in sports
- Goal setting and visualization
- Scholarship websites
- Recognizing scholarship scams
- Financial aid websites

Ask your instructor if you need any assistance in accessing the College Success website.

Endnotes

1. Quoted in Rob Gilbert, ed., *Bits and Pieces,* 4 November 1999, 15.
2. Alan Lakein, *How to Get Control of Your Time and Your Life* (New York: Peter H. Wyden, 1973).
3. Ibid., 70–71.
4. Dave Ellis, *Becoming a Master Student* (Boston: Houghton Mifflin, 1998).
5. Jane Burka and Lenora Yuen, *Procrastination* (Reading, MA: Addison-Wesley, 1983).
6. Frances Leonard, *Time Is Money*, (Addison-Wesley) cited in the *San Diego Union Tribune,* 14 October 1995.
7. Amy Dacyczyn, *The Tightwad Gazette II* (Villard Books), cited in the *San Diego Union Tribune,* 20 February 1995.
8. Jane Bryant Quinn, "Money Watch," *Good Housekeeping*, November 1996, 80.
9. Robert Hanley, "Breaking Bad Habits," *San Diego Union Tribune,* 7 September 1992.
10. Steven R. Covey, *The Seven Habits of Highly Effective People* (New York: Simon and Shuster, 1990), 150.

Test Taking

Chapter 4

Chapter Focus

Read to answer these key questions:

What are some test preparation techniques?   How should I review the material?   How can I predict the test questions?   What are some emergency test preparation techniques?   How can I deal with test anxiety?   How can I study math and deal with math anxiety?   What are some tips for taking objective tests?   How can I write a good essay?   What are some ideas for taking math tests?

An important skill for survival in college is the ability to take tests. Passing tests is also important in careers that require licenses, certificates, or continuing education. Knowing how to prepare for and take tests with confidence will help you to accomplish your educational and career goals while maintaining your good mental health. Once you have learned some basic test-taking and relaxation techniques, you can turn your test anxiety into motivation and good test results.

Preparing for Tests

Attend Every Class

The most significant factor in poor performance in college is lack of attendance. Students who attend the lectures and complete their assignments have the best chance for success in college. Attending the lectures help you to be involved in learning and to know what to expect on the test. College professors know that students who miss three classes in a row are not likely to return, and some professors drop students after three absences. After three absences, students can fall behind in their schoolwork and become overwhelmed with makeup work.

Distribute the Practice

The key to successful test preparation is to begin early and do a little at a time. Test preparation begins the first day of class. During the first class, the professor gives an overview of the course content, requirements, tests, and grading. These items are usually described in writing in the class calendar and syllabus. It is very important to attend the first class to get this important information. If you have to miss the first class, make sure to ask the professor for the syllabus and calendar and read it carefully.

From *College & Career Success*, 3rd edition by Marsha Fralick. Copyright © 2006 by Kendall/Hunt Publishing Company. Reprinted by permission.

Early test preparation helps you to take advantage of the powerful memory technique called distributed practice. In distributed practice, the material learned is broken up into small parts and reviewed frequently. Using this method can enable you to learn a large quantity of material without becoming overwhelmed. Here are some examples of using distributed practice:

- If you have a test on 50 Spanish vocabulary words in two weeks, don't wait until the day before the test to try to learn all 50 words. Waiting until the day before the test will result in difficulty remembering the words, test anxiety, and a dislike of studying Spanish. If you have 50 Spanish vocabulary words to learn in two weeks, learn five words each day and quickly review the words you learned previously. For example, on Monday you would learn five words and on Tuesday, you would learn five new words and review the ones learned on Monday. Give yourself the weekends off as a reward for planning ahead.
- If you have to read a history book with 400 pages, divide that number by the number of days in the semester or quarter. If there are 80 days in the semester, you will only have to read five pages per day or ten pages every other day. This is a much easier and more efficient way to master a long assignment.
- Don't wait until the last minute to study for a midterm or final exam. Keep up with the class each week. As you read each chapter, quickly review a previous chapter. In this way you can comfortably master the material. Just before a major test, you can review the material that you already know and feel confident about your ability to get a good grade on the test.

Schedule a Time and a Place for Studying

To take advantage of distributed practice, you will need to develop a study schedule. Write down your work time and school time and other scheduled activities. Identify times that can be used for studying each day. Get in the habit of using these available times for studying each week. As a general rule you need two hours of study time for each hour spent in a college classroom. If you cannot find enough time for studying, consider either reducing your course load or reducing work hours.

Use your study schedule or calendar to note the due dates of major projects and all test dates. Schedule enough time to complete projects and to finish major reviews for exams. Look at each due date and write in reminders to begin work or review well in advance of the due date. Give yourself plenty of time to meet the deadlines. It seems that around exam time, students are often ill or have problems that prevent them from being successful. Having some extra time scheduled will help you to cope with the many unexpected events that happen in everyday life.

Try to schedule your study sessions during your prime time, when you are awake and refreshed. For many people, one hour of study during the daylight hours is worth one and a half hours at night. Trying to study late at night may not be the best idea because it is difficult to motivate yourself to study when you are tired. Save the time at the end of the day for relaxing or doing routine chores.

Find a place to study. This can be an area of your home where you have a desk, computer, and all the necessary supplies for studying. As a general rule, do not study at the kitchen table, in front of the television, or in your bed. These places provide powerful cues for eating, watching television, or sleeping instead of studying. If you cannot find an appropriate place at home, use the college library as a place to study. The library is usually quiet and others are studying, so there are not too many distractions.

Test Review Tools

There are a variety of tools you can use to review for tests. Choose the tools according to your learning style and what works for you. Learning styles include visual, auditory, kinesthetic, and tactile modes of learning. **Visual learners** find it easy to make mental pictures of the material to be learned. **Auditory learners** prefer listening and reciting material out loud. **Kinesthetic learners** benefit from moving around or acting out material to be learned. **Tactile learners** benefit from physical activities such as writing down items to be remembered.

Flash cards. Flash cards are an effective way to learn facts and details for objective tests such as true-false, multiple-choice, matching, and fill-in-the-blank. For example, if you have 100 vocabulary words to learn in biology, put the word on one side and the definition on the other side. First, look at each definition and see if you can recall the word. If you are a visual learner, look at the word and see if you can recall the definition. If you are an auditory learner, say the words and definitions. If you are a tactile or kinesthetic learner, carry the cards with you and briefly look at them as you are going about your daily activities. Make a game of studying by sorting the cards into stacks of information you know and information you still have to practice. Work with flash cards frequently and review them quickly. Don't worry about learning all items at once. Each day that you practice, you will recall the items more easily.

> REVIEW TOOLS
> –Flash cards
> –Summary sheets
> –Mind maps
> –Study groups

Summary sheets. Summary sheets are used to record the key ideas from your lecture notes or textbook. It is important to be selective; write only the most important ideas on the summary sheets. At the end of the semester, you might have approximately ten pages of summary sheets from the text and ten pages from your notes. If you are a kinesthetic learner, writing down the items you wish to remember will help you learn them. If you are a visual learner, the summary sheet becomes a picture of the ideas you need to remember. If you are an auditory learner, recite aloud the important ideas on the summary sheets.

Mind maps. A mind map is a visual picture of the items you wish to remember. Start in the center of the page with a key idea and then surround it with related topics. You can use drawings, lines, circles, or colors to link and group the ideas. A mind map will help you to learn material in an organized way that will be useful when writing essay exams. (See chapter 5 for an example and more information on mind maps.)

Study groups. A study group is helpful in motivating yourself to learn through discussions of the material with other people. For the study group, select three to seven people who are motivated to be successful in class and can coordinate schedules. Study groups are often used in math and science classes. Groups of students work problems together and help each other understand the material. The study group is also useful in studying for exams. Give each member a part of the material to be studied. Have each person predict test questions and quiz the study group. Teaching the material to the study group can be the best way to learn it.

Reviewing Effectively

Begin your review early and break it into small parts. Remember that repetition is one of the effective ways to store information in long-term memory. Here are some types of review that help you to store information in long-term memory:

Immediate review. This type of review is fast and powerful and helps to minimize forgetting. It is the first step in storing information in long-term memory. Begin the process by turning each bold-faced heading in the text into a question. Read each section to answer the question you have asked. Read your college texts with a highlighter in hand so that you can mark the key ideas for review. Some students use a variety of colors to distinguish main ideas, supporting points, and key examples, for instance. When you are finished using the highlighter, quickly review the items you have marked. As you complete each section, quickly review the main points. When you finish the chapter, immediately review the key points in the entire chapter again. As soon as you finish taking your lecture notes, take a few minutes to review them. To be most effective, immediate review needs to occur as soon as possible or at least within the first twenty minutes of learning something.

Intermediate review. After you have finished reading and reviewing a new chapter in your textbook, spend a few minutes reviewing an earlier one. This step will help you to master the material and to recall it easily for the midterm or final exam. Another way to do intermediate review is to set up time periodically in your study schedule for reviewing previous chapters and classroom notes.

Final review. Before a major exam, organize your notes, materials, and assignments. Estimate how long it will take you to review the material. Break the material into manageable chunks. For an essay exam, use mind maps or summary sheets to write down the main points that you need to remember and recite these ideas frequently. For objective tests, use flash cards or lists to remember details and concepts that you expect to be on the test. Here is a sample seven-day plan for reviewing ten chapters for a final exam:

Day 1 Gather materials and study chapters 1 and 2 by writing key points on summary sheets or mind maps. Make flash cards of details you need to remember. Review and highlight lecture notes and handouts on these chapters.

Day 2 Review chapters 1 and 2. Study chapters 3 and 4 and the corresponding lecture notes.

Day 3 Review chapters 1 to 4. Study chapters 5 and 6 and the corresponding lecture notes.

Day 4 Review chapters 1 to 6. Study chapters 7 and 8 along with the corresponding lecture notes.

Day 5 Review chapters 1 to 8. Study chapters 9 and 10 along with corresponding lecture notes.

Day 6 Review notes, summary sheets, mind maps and flash cards for chapters 1 to 10. Relax and get a good night's sleep. You are well prepared.

Day 7 Do one last quick review of chapters 1 to 10 and walk into the test with the confidence that you will be successful on the exam.

Predicting Test Questions

There are many ways to predict the questions that will be on the test. Here are some ideas that might be helpful:

- Look for clues from the professor about what will be on the test. Many times the professors put information about the tests on the course syllabus. During lectures, they often give hints about what will be important to know. If a professor repeats something more than once, make note of it as a possible test question. Anything written on the board is likely to be on the test. Sometimes the professor will even say, "This will be on the test." Write these important points in your notes and review them.
- College textbooks are usually written in short sections with bold headings. Turn each bold-faced heading into a question and read to answer the question. Understand and review the main idea in each section. The test questions will generally address the main ideas in the text.

- Don't forget to study and review the handouts that the professor distributes to the class. If the professor has taken the time and effort to provide extra material, it is probably important and may be on the test.
- Form a study group and divide up the material to be reviewed. Have each member of the group write some test questions based on the important points in each main section of the text. When the study group meets, take turns asking likely test questions and providing the answers.
- When the professor announces the test, make sure to ask what material is to be covered on the test and what kind of test it is. If necessary, ask the professor which concepts are most important. Know what kind of test questions will be asked (essay, true-false, multiple-choice, matching, or short-answer). Some professors may provide sample exams or math problems.
- Use the first test to understand what is expected and how to study for future tests.

Preparing for an Open–Book Test

In college you may have some open-book tests. Open-book tests are often used in very technical subjects where specific material from the book is needed to answer questions. For example, in an engineering course, tables and formulas in the book may be needed to solve engineering problems on an exam. To study for an open-book test, focus on understanding the material and being able to locate key information for the exam. Consider making index tabs for your book so that you can locate needed information quickly. Be sure to bring your book, calculator, and other needed material to the exam.

Emergency Procedures

If it is a day or two before the test and you have not followed the above procedures, it is time for the college practice known as "cramming." There are two main problems that result from this practice. First you cannot take advantage of distributed practice, so it will be difficult to remember large amounts of material. Second it is not fun, and if done often will result in anxiety and a dislike of education. Because of these problems, some students who rely on cramming wrongly conclude that they are not capable of finishing their education.

If you must cram for a test, here are some emergency procedures that may be helpful in getting the best grade possible under difficult circumstances:

- When cramming *it is most important to be selective*. Try to identify the main points and recite and review them.
- Focus on reviewing and reciting the lecture notes. In this way, you will cover the main ideas the professor thinks are important.
- If you have not read the text, skim and search each chapter looking for the main points. Highlight and review these main points. Read the chapter summaries. In a math textbook, practice sample problems.
- Make summary sheets containing the main ideas from the notes and the text. Recite and review the summary sheets.
- For objective tests, focus on learning new terms and vocabulary related to the subject. These terms are likely to be on the test. Flash cards are helpful.
- For essay tests, develop an outline of major topics and review the outline so you can write an essay.
- Get enough rest. Staying up all night to review for the test can result in confusion, reduced mental ability, and test anxiety.
- Hope for the best.
- Plan ahead next time so that you can get a better grade.

If you have very little time to review for a test, you will probably experience information overload. One strategy for dealing with this problem is based on the work of George Miller of Harvard University. He found that the optimum chunks of information that we can remember is seven plus or minus two (or five to nine chunks of information).[1] This is also known as the Magical Number Seven Theory. For this last-minute review technique, start with five sheets of paper. Next, identify five key concepts that are likely to be on the test. Write one concept on the top of each sheet of paper. Then check your notes and text to write an explanation, definition, or answer for each of these topics. If you have more time, find two to four more concepts and research them, writing the information on additional sheets. You should have no more than nine sheets of paper. Arrange the sheets in order of importance. Review and recite the key ideas on these sheets. Get a regular night's sleep before the test and do some relaxation exercises right before the test.

Ideas That Don't Work

Some students do poorly on tests for the following reasons.

- Attending a party or social event the evening before a major test rather than doing the final review will adversely affect your test score. Study in advance and reward yourself with the party after the test.
- Skipping the major review before the test may cause you to forget some important material.
- Taking drugs or drinking alcohol before a test may give you the impression that you are relaxed and doing well on the test, but the results are disastrous to your success on the exam and your good health.
- Not knowing the date of the test can cause you to get a low grade because you are not prepared.
- Not checking or knowing about the final exam schedule can cause you to miss the final.
- Missing the final exam can result in a lower grade or failing the class.
- Arriving late for the exam puts you at a disadvantage if you don't have time to finish or have to rush through the test.
- Deciding not to buy or read the textbook will cause low performance or failure.
- Having a fight, disagreement, or argument with parents, friends, or significant others before the test will make it difficult to focus on the exam.
- Sacrificing sleep, exercise, or food to prepare for the exam makes it difficult to do your best.
- Cheating on an exam can cause embarrassment, a lower grade, or failure. It can even lead to expulsion from college.
- Missing the exam because you are not prepared and asking the professor to let you make up the exam later is a tactic that many students try. Most professors will not permit you to take an exam late.
- Inventing a creative excuse for missing an exam is so common that some professors have a collection of these stories that they share with colleagues. Creative excuses don't work with most professors.
- Arriving at the exam without the proper materials such as a pencil, scantron, paper, calculator, or book (for open-book exams) can cause you to miss the exam or start the exam late.

Dealing with Test Anxiety

Some anxiety is a good thing. It can provide motivation to study and prepare for exams. However, it is common for college students to suffer from test anxiety. Too much anxiety can lower your performance on tests. Some symptoms of test anxiety include:

- Fear of failing a test even though you are well prepared
- Physical symptoms such as perspiring, increased heart rate, shortness of breath, upset stomach, tense muscles, or headache
- Negative thoughts about the test and your grade
- Mental blocking of material you know and remembering it once you leave the exam

You can minimize your test anxiety by being well prepared and by applying the memory strategies described in earlier chapters. Prepare for your exams by attending every class, keeping up with your reading assignments, and reviewing during the semester. These steps will help increase your self-confidence and reduce anxiety. Apply the principles of memory improvement to your studying. As you are reading, find the important points and highlight them. Review these points so that they are stored in your long-term memory. Use distributed practice and spread out learning over time rather than trying to learn it all at once. Visualize and organize what you need to remember. Trust in your abilities and intend to remember what you have studied.

If you find that you are anxious, here are some ideas you can try to cope with the anxiety. Experiment with these techniques to see which ones work best for you.

- **Do some physical exercise.** Physical exercise helps to use up stress hormones. Make physical activity a part of your daily routine. Arrive for your test a little early and walk briskly around campus for about twenty minutes. This exercise will help you to feel relaxed and energized.
- **Get a good night's sleep before the test.** Lack of sleep can interfere with memory and cause irritability, anxiety, and confusion.
- **Take deep breaths.** Immediately before the test, take a few deep breaths; hold them for three to five seconds and let them out slowly. These deep breaths will help you to relax and keep a sufficient supply of oxygen in your blood. Oxygen is needed for proper brain function.
- **Visualize and rehearse your success.** Begin by getting as comfortable and relaxed as possible in your favorite chair or lying down in bed. Visualize yourself walking into the exam room. Try to imagine the room in as much detail as possible. If possible, visit the exam room before the test so that you can get a good picture of it. See yourself taking the exam calmly and confidently. You know most of the answers. If you find a question you do not know, see yourself circling it and coming back to it later. Imagine that you find a clue on the test that triggers your recall of the answers to the difficult questions. Picture yourself handing in the exam with a good feeling about doing well on the test. Then imagine you are getting the test back and you get a good grade on the test. You congratulate yourself for a job well done. If you suffer from text anxiety, you may need to rehearse this scene several times. When you enter the exam room, the visual picture that you have rehearsed will help you to relax.
- **Acknowledge your anxiety.** The first step in dealing with anxiety is to admit that you are anxious rather than trying to fight it or deny it. Say to yourself, "I am feeling anxious." Take a few deep breaths and then focus your attention on the test.
- **Do the easy questions first** and mark the ones that may be difficult. This will help you to relax. Once you are relaxed, the difficult questions become more manageable.
- **Yell "Stop."** Negative and frightening thoughts can cause anxiety. Here are some examples of negative thoughts:

TIPS TO MINIMIZE ANXIETY

–Exercise
–Sleep
–Take deep breaths
–Visualize success
–Acknowledge anxiety
–Easy questions first
–Yell "Stop!"
–Daydream
–Practice perspective
–Give yourself time
–Get help

I'm going to fail this test.
I don't know the answer to number ten!
I never do well on tests.
Essays! I have a hard time with those.
I'll never make it through college.
I was never any good in math!

These types of thoughts don't help you do better on the test, so stop saying them. They cause you to become anxious and to freeze up during the test. If you find yourself with similar thoughts, yell "stop" to yourself. This will cause you to interrupt your train of thought so that you can think about the task at hand rather than becoming more anxious. Replace negative thoughts with more positive ones such as these:

I'm doing the best I can.
I am well prepared and know most of the answers.
I don't know the answer to number ten, so I'll just circle it and come back to it later.
I'll make an outline in the margin for the essay question.
College is difficult, but I'll make it!
Math is a challenge, but I can do it!

- **Daydream.** Think about being in your favorite place. Take time to think about the details. Allow yourself to be there for a while until you feel more relaxed.
- **Practice perspective.** Remember, one poor grade is not the end of the world. It does not define who you are. If you do not do well, think about how you can improve your preparation and performance the next time.
- **Give yourself time.** Test anxiety develops over a period of time. It will take some time to get over it. Learn the best ways to prepare for the exam and practice saying positive thoughts to yourself.
- **Get help.** If these techniques do not work for you, seek help from your college health or counseling center.

Studying Math and Dealing with Math Anxiety

When I mention to students that they need to take math, I often see a look of fear on their faces. Everyone needs to take math. Most colleges require math classes and demonstrated math competency in order to graduate. Math is essential for many high-paying technical and professional occupations. Being afraid of math and avoiding it will limit your career possibilities.

Begin your study of math with some positive thinking. You may have had difficulty with math in the past, but with a positive attitude and the proper study techniques, you can meet the challenge. The first step to success in math is to put in the effort required. Attend class, do your homework, and get help if needed. If you put in the effort and hard work, you will gain experience in math. If you gain experience with math, you will become more confident in your ability to do math. If you have confidence, you will gain satisfaction in doing math. You may even learn to like it! If you like the subject, you can gain competence. The process looks like this:

Hard work → Experience → Confidence → Satisfaction → Competence

Although you may have had difficulty with math in the past, you can become successful by following these steps. Your reward is self-satisfaction and increased opportunity in technical and professional careers.

- **Don't delay taking math.** You may need a sequence of math courses in order to graduate. If you delay taking math, you may delay your graduation from college.
- **Think positively about your ability to succeed in math.** You may have had difficulties in math classes before. Think about your educational history. Can you recall having difficulties in the past? These past difficulties cause a fear of math. You may have a picture of failure in your mind. You need to replace it with a picture of success. Acknowledge that you are afraid because of past experiences with math. Acknowledge that the future can be different, and spend the time and effort needed to be successful.
- **Start at the beginning.** Assess where your math skills are at the present time. If you have not taken math classes for some time, you may need to review. Take the college math assessment test, read the college catalog, and speak to a counselor about where you should start.
- **Ask questions in class.** Students are often afraid to ask questions in math classes because they are afraid other students will think they are not smart. It is more likely that other students are wishing that someone would ask a question because they don't understand either. Ask your questions early, as soon as you find something you don't understand.
- **Get help early.** If you are having difficulties, get tutoring right away. If you are confused, you will not understand the next step either.
- **Don't miss your math classes.** It is difficult to catch up if you miss class.
- **Do your math homework regularly.** Math skills depend on practice. Make sure you understand the examples given in the textbook. Practice as many questions as you can until you feel comfortable solving the problems. Assign yourself extra problems if necessary. It is difficult to cram for a math test.
- **Use a study group.** Work with groups of students to study math. Get the phone number of other students in the study group. If you do not understand, other students may be able to help.
- **Study for the math test.** Start early so that you will have time to go over each topic in the book and practice doing problems from each section. Check your work against the solutions given in the text.
- **Do the easiest problems first on a math test.** In this way, you can gain confidence and relax. Then focus on the problems that are worth the most points. Don't be distracted by problems that you do not know and that use up test time.
- **Solve problems systematically.** First make sure you understand the problem. Write out the given facts and equations you may need to use before working out the problem. Then make a plan for solving it. What have you learned in class that will help you to solve the problem? Carry out the plan. Then check your answer. Does the answer make sense? Check your calculator work over again at the end of the test.
- **Check for careless errors.** Go over your math test to see if you have made any careless errors. Forgetting a plus or minus sign or adding or subtracting incorrectly can have a big impact on your grade. Save at least five minutes to read over your test.
- **Get enough sleep before the math test.** If you are mentally sharp, the test will be easier.

Test Preparation

Test what you have learned by selecting the correct answer to the following questions.

1. In test preparation, it is important to use this memory technique.
   A. Distribute the practice.
   B. Read every chapter just before the test.
   C. Do most of the review right before the test to minimize forgetting.

2. Schedule your study sessions
   A. late at night.
   B. during your prime time, which is generally earlier in the day.
   C. after all other activities are done.

3. Effective tools to learn facts and details are
   A. mind maps.
   B. summary sheets.
   C. flash cards.

4. The best way to review is
   A. to start early and break it into small parts.
   B. immediately before the test.
   C. in large blocks of time.

5. The best way to deal with text anxiety is to
   A. visualize your failure on the exam.
   B. start with the difficult questions first.
   C. be well prepared and visualize your success on the exam.

How did you do on the quiz? Check your answers: 1. A, 2. B, 3. C, 4. A, 5. C

Taking Tests

True–False Tests

Many professors use objective tests such as true-false and multiple-choice because of their ease in grading. The best way to prepare for these types of tests is to study the key points in the textbook, lecture notes, and class handouts. In the textbook, take each bold-faced topic and turn it into a question. If you can answer the question, you will be successful on objective tests.

In addition to studying for the test, it is helpful to understand some basic test-taking techniques that will help you to determine the correct answer. Many of the techniques used to determine whether a statement is true or false can also be used to eliminate wrong answers on multiple-choice tests.

To develop strategies for success on true-false exams, it is important to understand how a teacher writes the questions. For a true-false question, the teacher identifies a key point in the book or lecture notes. Then he or she has two choices. For a true statement, the key idea is often written exactly as it appears in the text or notes. For a false statement, the key idea is changed in some way to make it false.

One way to make a statement false is to add a **qualifier** to the statement. Qualifiers that are *absolute* or extreme are generally, but not always, found in false statements. *General* qualifiers are often found in true statements.

Ten Rules for Success

Here are ten rules for success on any test. Are there any new ideas you can put into practice?

1. Make sure to set your alarm, and consider having a backup in case your alarm doesn't go off. Set a second alarm or have someone call to make sure you are awake on time.
2. Arrive a little early for your exam. If you are taking a standardized test like the Scholastic Aptitude Test (SAT) or Graduate Record Exam (GRE), familiarize yourself with the location of the exam. If you arrive early, you can take a quick walk around the building to relax or spend a few minutes doing a review so that your brain will be tuned up and ready.
3. Eat a light breakfast including some carbohydrates and protein. Be careful about eating sugar and caffeine before a test because this can contribute to greater anxiety and low blood sugar by the time you take the test. The worst breakfast would be something like a doughnut and coffee or a soda and candy bar. Examples of good breakfasts are eggs, toast, and juice or cereal with milk and fruit.
4. Think positively about the exam. Tell yourself that you are well prepared and the exam is an opportunity to show what you know.
5. Make sure you have the proper materials: scantrons, paper, pencil or pen, calculator, books and notes (for open-book exams).
6. Manage your time. Know how long you have for the test and then scan the test to make a time management plan. For example, if you have one hour and there are 50 objective questions, you have about a minute for each question. Half way through the time, you should have completed 25 questions. If there are three essay questions in an hour, you have less than 20 minutes for each question. Save some time to look over the test and make corrections.
7. Neatness is important. If your paper looks neat, the professor is more likely to have a positive attitude about the paper before it is even read. If the paper is hard to read, the professor will start reading your paper with a negative attitude, possibly resulting in a lower grade.
8. Read the test directions carefully. On essay exams, it is common for the professor to give you a choice of questions to answer. If you do not read the directions, you may try to answer all of the questions and then run out of time or give incomplete answers to them.
9. If you get stuck on a difficult question, don't worry about it. Just mark it and find an easier question. You may find clues on the rest of the test that will aid your recall or you may be more relaxed later on and think of the answer.
10. Be careful not to give any impression that you might be cheating. Keep your eyes on your own paper. If you have memory aids or outlines memorized, write them directly on the test paper rather than a separate sheet so that you are not suspected of using cheat notes.

Absolute Qualifiers (false)		*General Qualifiers (true)*	
all	none	usually	frequently
always	never	often	sometimes
only	nobody	some	seldom
invariably	no one	many	much
best	worst	most	generally
everybody	everyone	few	ordinarily
absolutely	absolutely not	probably	a majority
certainly	certainly not	might	a few
no	every	may	apt to

SEVEN TIPS FOR SUCCESS ON TRUE–FALSE TESTS

1. **Identify the key ideas in the text and class notes and review them.**
2. **Accept the question at face value.** Don't overanalyze or create wild exceptions in your mind.

3. **If you don't know the answer, assume it is true.** There are generally more true statements because we all like the truth (especially teachers) and true questions are easier to write. However, some teachers like to test students by writing all false statements.
4. **If any part of a true-false statement is false, the whole statement is false.** Carefully read each statement to determine if any part of it is false. Students sometimes assume a statement is true if most of it is true. This is not correct.

   Example: Good relaxation techniques include deep breathing, exercise, and visualizing your failure on the exam.

   This statement is false because visualizing failure can lead to test anxiety and failure.

5. **Notice any absolute or general qualifiers.** Remember that absolute qualifiers often make a statement false. General qualifiers often make a statement true.

   Example: The student who crams **always** does poorly on the exam.

   This statement is false because **some** students are successful at cramming for an exam.

   Be careful with this rule. Sometimes the answer can be absolute.

   Example: The grade point average is always calculated by dividing the number of units attempted by the grade points. (true)

6. **Notice words such as *because*, *therefore*, *consequently*, and *as a result*.** They may connect two things that are true but result in a false statement.

   Example: Martha does not have test anxiety. (true)

   Martha makes good grades on tests. (true)

   Martha does not have test anxiety and therefore makes good grades on tests.

   This statement is false because she also has to prepare for the exam. Not having test anxiety could even cause her to lack motivation to study and do poorly on a test.

7. **Watch for double negatives.** Two no's equal a yes. If you see two negatives in a sentence, read them as a positive. Be careful with negative prefixes such as: un-, im-, mis-, dis-, il-, and ir-. For example, the phrase "not uncommon" actually means "common." Notice that the word "not" and the prefix "un-" when used together form a double negative that equals a positive.

   Example: **Not** being **un**prepared for the test is the best way to earn good grades.

   The above sentence is confusing. To make it clearer, change both of the negatives into a positive:

   Being prepared for the test is the best way to earn good grades.

Activity   Practice True-False Test

Answer the following questions by applying the tips for success in the previous section. Place a T or an F in the blanks.

_____ 1. If a statement has an absolute qualifier, it is always false.

_____ 2. Statements with general qualifiers are frequently true.

_____ 3. If you don't know the answer, you should guess true.

_____ 4. Studying the key points for true-false tests is not unimportant.

_____ 5. Good test-taking strategies include eating a light breakfast that includes carbohydrates and protein and drinking plenty of coffee to stay alert.

_____ 6. Ryan attended every class this semester and therefore earned an A in the class.

How did you do on the test?

Answers: 1. F, 2. T, 3. T, 4. T, 5. F, 6. F

Multiple-Choice Tests

College exams often include multiple-choice questions rather than true-false questions because it is more difficult to guess the correct answer. On a true-false exam, the student has a 50 percent chance of guessing the correct answer while on a multiple-choice question the odds of guessing correctly are only 25 percent. You can think of a multiple-choice question as four true-false questions in a row. First, read the question and try to answer it without looking at the options. This will help you to focus on the question and determine the correct answer. Look at each option and determine if it is true or false. Then choose the *best* answer.

To choose the best option, it is helpful to understand how a teacher writes a multiple-choice question. Here are the steps a teacher uses to write a multiple-choice exam:

1. Find an important point in the lecture notes, text, or handouts.
2. Write a **stem**. This is an incomplete statement or a question.
3. Write the correct answer as one of the options.
4. Write three or four plausible but incorrect options that might be chosen by students who are not prepared. These incorrect options are called **decoys**. Here is an example:

    Stem: If you are anxious about taking math tests, it is helpful to

    A. Stay up the night before the test to review thoroughly. (**decoy**)
    B. Visualize yourself doing poorly on the test so you will be motivated to study. (**decoy**)
    C. Practice math problems regularly during the semester. (**correct answer**)
    D. Do the most difficult problem first. (**decoy**)

Being well prepared for the test is the most reliable way of recognizing the correct answer and the decoys. In addition, becoming familiar with the following rules for recognizing decoys can help you determine the correct answer or improve your chances of guessing the correct answer on an exam. If you can at least eliminate some of the wrong answers, you will improve your odds of selecting the correct answer.

Rules for recognizing a decoy or wrong answer:

1. **The decoys are all true or all false statements.** Read each option and determine which options are false and which statements are true. This will help you to find the correct answer.

    Example: To manage your time on a test, it is important to

    A. Skip the directions and work as quickly as possible. (false)
    B. Skim through the test to see how much time you have for each section. (true)

C. Do the most difficult sections first. (false)
D. Just start writing as quickly as possible. (false)

Read the stem carefully because sometimes you will be asked to identify one false statement in a group of true statements.

> **Rules for Recognizing a Decoy**
> 1. Decoys are all true or all false
> 2. Decoys contain absolute qualifiers
> 3. Decoys can be partly true
> 4. Decoys have conjunctions that make them false
> 5. Decoys have double negatives
> 6. Decoys can be foolish
> 7. Decoys are high or low numbers
> 8. Decoys can look correct
> 9. Decoys are often the shorter answer
> 10. Decoys may be grammatically incorrect
> 11. Decoys may be an opposite
> 12. Decoys may be the same as another answer

2. **The decoy may contain an absolute qualifier.** The option with the absolute qualifier (e.g., always, only, every) is likely to be false because few things in life are absolute. There are generally exceptions to any rule.
3. **The decoy can be partly true.** However, if one part of the statement is false, the whole statement is false and an incorrect answer.
4. **The decoy may have a conjunction or other linking words that makes it false.** Watch for words and phrases such as *because, consequently, therefore,* and *as a result*.
5. **The decoy may have a double negative.** Having two negatives in a sentence makes it difficult to understand. Read the two negatives as a positive.
6. **The decoy may be a foolish option.** Writing multiple decoys is difficult, so test writers sometimes throw in foolish or humorous options.

   Example: In a multiple-choice test, a decoy is

   A. a type of duck.
   B. an incorrect answer.
   C. a type of missile used in air defense.
   D. a type of fish.

   The correct answer is B. Sometimes students are tempted by the foolish answers.

7. **The decoy is often a low or high number.** If you have a multiple-choice question with numbers, and you are not sure of the correct answer, choose the number in the middle range. It is often more likely to be correct.

   Example: George Miller of Harvard University theorized that the optimum number of chunks of material that we can remember is:

   A. 1–2 (This low number is a decoy)
   B. 5–9 (correct answer)
   C. 10–12 (close to the correct answer)
   D. 20–25 (This high number is a decoy)

   There is an exception to this rule when the number is much higher or lower than the average person thinks is possible.

8. **The decoy may look like the correct answer.** When two options look alike, one is incorrect and the other may be the correct answer. Test writers often use words that look alike as decoys.

   Example: In false statements, the qualifier is often

   A. absolute.
   B. resolute.
   C. general.
   D. exaggerated.

   The correct answer is A. Answer B is an incorrect look-alike option.

9. **Decoys are often shorter than the correct answer.** Longer answers are more likely to be correct because they are more complete. Avoid choosing the first answer that seems to be correct. There may be a better and more complete answer.

Example: Good test preparation involves
   A. doing the proper review for the test.
   B. good time management.
   C. a positive attitude.
   D. having good attendance, studying and reviewing regularly, being able to deal with test anxiety, and having a positive mental attitude.

Option D is correct because it is the most complete and thus the best answer.

10. **Decoys may be grammatically incorrect.** The correct answer will fit the grammar of the stem. A stem ending with "a" will match an answer beginning with a consonant; stems ending with "an" will match a word beginning with a vowel. The answer will agree in gender, number, and person with the stem.

    Example: In test taking, a decoy is an
       A. incorrect answer.
       B. correct answer.
       C. false answer.
       D. true answer.

The correct answer is A. It is also the only answer that grammatically fits with the stem. Also note that decoys can be all true or all false. In standardized tests, the grammar is usually correct. On teacher-made tests, the grammar can be a clue to the correct answer.

11. **A decoy is sometimes an opposite.** When two options are opposites, one is incorrect and the other is sometimes, but not always, correct.

    Example: A decoy is
       A. a right answer.
       B. a wrong answer.
       C. a general qualifier.
       D. a true statement.

The two opposites are answers A and B. The correct answer is B.

12. **A decoy may be the same as another answer.** If two answers say the same thing in different ways, they are both decoys and incorrect.

    Example: A true statement is likely to have this type of qualifier:
       A. extreme
       B. absolute
       C. general
       D. factual

Notice that answers A and B are the same and are incorrect. The correct answer is C.

    Example: How much does a gallon of water weigh?
       A. 8.34 pounds
       B. 5.5 pounds
       C. 5 pounds 8 ounces
       D. 20 pounds

B and C are the same and are therefore incorrect answers. Answer D is a high number. The correct answer is A.

If you are unable to identify any decoys, these suggestions may be helpful:

- Mark the question and come back to it later. You may find the answer elsewhere on the test or some words that help you remember the answer. After answering some easier questions, you may be able to relax and remember the answer.
- Trust your intuition and choose something that sounds familiar.
- Do not change your first answer unless you have misread the question or are sure that the answer is incorrect. Sometimes students overanalyze a question and then choose the wrong answer.
- The option "All of the above" is often correct because it is easier to write true statements rather than false ones. Options like A and B, B and D, or other combinations are also likely to be correct for the same reason.
- If you have no idea about the correct answer, guess option B or C. Most correct answers are in the middle.

Activity   Practice Multiple-Choice Test

Circle the letter of the correct answer. Then check your answers using the key at the end of this section.

1. The correct answer in a multiple-choice question is likely to be
   A. the shortest answer.
   B. the longest and most complete answer.
   C. the answer with an absolute qualifier.
   D. the answer that has some truth in it.

2. When guessing on a question involving numbers, it is generally best to
   A. choose the highest number.
   B. choose the lowest number.
   C. choose the mid-range number.
   D. always choose the first option.

3. If you have test anxiety, what questions should you answer first on the test?
   A. The most difficult questions
   B. The easiest questions
   C. The questions at the beginning
   D. The questions worth the least points

4. When taking a multiple-choice test, you should
   A. pick the first choice that is true.
   B. read all the choices and select the best one.
   C. pick the first choice that is false.
   D. choose the extreme answer.

5. A good method for guessing is to
   A. identify which choices are true and false.
   B. use the process of elimination.
   C. notice absolute qualifiers and conjunctions.
   D. all of the above.

6. The key to success when taking a multiple-choice test is
   A. cheating.
   B. good preparation.
   C. knowing how to guess.
   D. being able to recognize a qualifier.

7. The following rule about decoys is correct:
   A. A decoy is always absolute.
   B. A decoy can be partly true.
   C. Every decoy has a qualifier.
   D. Decoys are invariably false statements.

8. An example of an absolute qualifier is
   A. generally.
   B. never.
   C. sometimes.
   D. frequently.

9. Statements with absolute qualifiers are generally
   A. true.
   B. false.
   C. irrelevant.
   D. confusing.

10. If two multiple-choice options are the same or very similar, they are most likely
    A. decoys.
    B. a correct answer.
    C. a true answer.
    D. a mistake on the test.

11. It is generally not a good idea to change your answer unless
    A. you are very anxious about the test.
    B. you do not have good intuition.
    C. you notice that your intelligent friend has a different answer.
    D. you have misread the question and you are sure that the answer is incorrect.

Answers:

1. B, 2. C, 3. B, 4. B, 5. D, 6. B, 7. B (notice the absolute qualifiers in the decoys), 8. B, 9. B (notice the opposites), 10. A (notice the grammar), 11. D

Matching Tests

A matching test involves two lists of facts or definitions that must be matched together. Here are some tips to help you successfully complete a matching exam:

1. Read through both lists to discover the pattern or relationship between the lists. The lists might give words and definitions, people and accomplishments, or other paired facts.
2. Count the items on the list of answers to see if there is only one match for each item or if there are some extra answer choices.
3. Start with one list and match the items that you know. In this way, you have a better chance of guessing on the items that you do not know.
4. If you have difficulty with some of the items, leave them blank and return later. You may find the answers or clues on the rest of the test.

Activity Practice Matching Test

Match the items in the first column with the items in the second column. Write the letter of the matching item in the blank at the left.

_____ 1. Meaningful organization   A. Learn small amounts and review frequently.

_____ 2. Visualization   B. The more you know, the easier it is to remember.

_____ 3. Recitation   C. Tell yourself you will remember.

_____ 4. Develop an interest   D. Pretend you like it.

_____ 5. See the big picture   E. Make a mental picture.

_____ 6. Intend to remember   F. Rehearse and review.

_____ 7. Distribute the practice   G. Focus on the main points first.

_____ 8. Create a basic background   H. Personal organization.

Answers: 1. H, 2. E, 3. F, 4. D, 5. G, 6. C, 7. A, 8. B

Sentence-Completion or Fill-in-the-Blank Tests

Fill-in-the-blank and sentence-completion tests are more difficult than true-false or multiple-choice tests because they require the *recall* of specific information rather than the *recognition* of the correct answer. To prepare for this type of test, focus on facts such as definitions, names, dates, and places. Using flash cards to prepare can be helpful. For example, to memorize names, place the name on one side of the card and some identifying words on the other side. Practice looking at the names on one side of the card and then recalling the identifying words on the other side of the card. Then turn the cards over and look at the identifying words to recall the names.

Sometimes the test has clues that will help you to fill in the blank. Clues can include the length of the blanks and the number of blanks. Find an answer that makes sense in the sentence and matches the grammar of the sentence. If you cannot think of an answer, write a general description and you may get partial credit. Look for clues on the rest of the test that may trigger your recall.

Activity Practice Fill-in-the-Blank Test

Complete each sentence with the appropriate word or words.

1. Fill-in-the-blank tests are more difficult because they depend on the _____ of specific information.

2. On a true-false test, a statement is likely to be false if it contains an _____ qualifier.

3. Test review tools include _____, _____, and _____.

4. When studying for tests, visualize your _____.

Answers: 1. recall, 2. absolute, 3. flash cards, summary sheets, and mind maps (also study groups and highlighters), 4. success

Essay Tests

Many professors choose essay questions because they are the best way to show what you have learned in the class. Essay questions can be challenging because you not only have to know the material but must be able to organize it and use good writing techniques in your answer.

Essay questions contain key words that will guide you in writing your answer. One of the keys to success in writing answers to essay questions is to note these key words and then structure your essay accordingly. As you read through an essay question, look for these words:

Analyze	Break into separate parts and discuss, examine, or interpret each part.
Argue	State an opinion and give reasons for the opinion.
Comment	Give your opinion.
Compare	Identify two or more ideas and identify similarities and differences.
Contrast	Show how the components are the same or different.
Criticize	Give your opinion and make judgments.
Defend	State reasons.
Define	Give the meaning of the word or concept as used within the course of study.
Describe	Give a detailed account or provide information.
Demonstrate	Provide evidence.
Diagram	Make a drawing, chart, graph, sketch, or plan.
Differentiate	Tell how the ideas are the same and how they are different.
Describe	Make a picture with words. List the characteristics, qualities and parts.
Discuss	Describe the pros and cons of the issues. Compare and contrast.
Enumerate	Make a list of ideas, events, qualities, reasons, and so on.
Explain	Make an idea clear. Show how and why.
Evaluate	Describe it and give your opinion about something.
Illustrate	Give concrete examples and explain them. Draw a diagram.
Interpret	Say what something means. Describe and then evaluate.
Justify	Prove a point. Give the reasons why.
Outline	Describe the main ideas.
Prove	Support with facts. Give evidence or reasons.
Relate	Show the connections between ideas or events.
State	Explain precisely. Provide the main points.
Summarize	Give a brief, condensed account. Draw a conclusion.
Trace	Show the order of events.

Here are some tips on writing essays:

1. To prepare for an essay test, use a mind map or summary sheet to summarize the main ideas. Organize the material in the form of an outline or mental pictures that you can use in writing.
2. The first step in writing an essay is to quickly survey the test and read the directions carefully. Many times you are offered a choice of which and how many questions to answer.
3. Manage your time. Note how many questions need to be answered and how many points each question is worth.

    For example, if you have three questions to answer in one hour, you will have less than 20 minutes for each question. Save some time to check over your work.

    If the questions are worth different points, divide up your time proportionately. In the above example with three questions, if one question is worth 50 points and the other two are worth 25 points, spend half the time on the 50-point question (less than 30 minutes) and divide the remaining time between the 25-point questions (less than 15 minutes each).
4. If you are anxious about the test, start with an easy question in order to relax and build your confidence. If you are confident of your test-taking abilities, start with the question that is worth the most points.
5. Get organized. Write a brief outline in the margin of your test paper. Do not write your outline on a separate sheet of paper because you may be accused of using cheat notes.
6. In the first sentence of your essay, rephrase the question and provide a direct answer. Rephrasing the question keeps you on track and a direct answer becomes the thesis statement or main idea of the essay.

    Example: (Question:) Describe a system for reading a college textbook.

    (Answer:) A system for reading a college textbook is Survey, Question, Read, Review, Recite, and Reflect (SQ4R). (Then you would go on to expand on each part of the topic.)
7. Use the principles of good composition. Start with a thesis statement or main idea. Provide supporting ideas and examples to support your thesis. Provide a brief summary at the end.
8. Write your answer clearly and neatly so it is easy to grade. Grading an essay involves an element of subjectivity. If your paper looks neat and is easy to read, the professor is likely to read your essay with a positive attitude. If your paper is difficult to read, the professor will probably read your paper with a negative attitude.
9. Determine the length of your essay by the number of points it is worth. For example, a five-point essay might be a paragraph with five key points. A 25-point essay would probably be a five-paragraph essay with at least 25 key points.
10. Save some time at the end to read over your essays. Make corrections, make sure your answers make sense, and add any key information you may have forgotten to include.

Math Tests

Taking a math test involves some different strategies:

1. Some instructors will let you write down some formulas on an index card or a small crib sheet. Prepare these notes carefully, writing down the key formulas you will need for the exam.

2. If you have to memorize formulas, review them right before the test and write them on the test immediately.
3. As a first step, quickly look over the test. Find a problem you can solve easily and do this problem first.
4. Manage your time. Find out how many problems you have to solve and how much time is available for each problem. Do the problems worth the most points first. Stay on track.
5. Try this four step process:
   A. Understand the problem.
   B. Devise a plan to solve the problem. Write down the information that is given. Think about the skills and techniques you have learned in class that can help you to solve the problem.
   C. Carry out the plan.
   D. Look back to see if your answer is reasonable.
6. If you cannot work a problem, go on to the next question. Come back later when you are more relaxed. If you spend too much time on a problem you cannot work, you will not have time for the problems that you can work.
7. Even if you think an answer is wrong, turn it in. You may get partial credit.
8. Show all the steps in your work and label your answer. On long and complex problems, it is helpful to use short sentences to explain your steps in solving the problem.
9. Estimate your answer and see if it makes sense or is logical.
10. Write your numbers as neatly as possible to avoid mistakes and to make them legible for the professor.
11. Leave space between your answers in case you need to add to them later.
12. If you have time left over at the end, recheck your answers.

What to Do When Your Test Is Returned

When your test is returned, use it as feedback for future test preparation in the course. Look at your errors and try to determine how to prevent these errors in the future.

- Did you study correctly?
- Did you study the proper materials?
- Did you use the proper test-taking techniques?
- Was the test more difficult than you expected?
- Did you run out of time to take the test?
- Was the test focused on details and facts or on general ideas and principles?
- Did you have problems with test anxiety?

Analyzing your test performance can help you to do better in the future.

Be Prepared

The key idea in this chapter is to be prepared. Good preparation is essential for success in test taking as well as in many other areas of life. Being successful begins with having a vision of the future and then taking steps to achieve your dream.

> *The secret of getting ahead is getting started. The secret of getting started is breaking your complex, overwhelming tasks into small manageable tasks, and then starting on the first one.*
>
> —Mark Twain

Sometimes people think of success in terms of good luck. Thomas Jefferson said, "I'm a great believer in luck, and I find the harder I work, the more I have of it." Don't depend on good luck. Work to create your success.

You can reach your dream of attaining a college education through preparation and hard work. Use the ideas in this chapter to ensure your success. Remember that preparation begins on the first day of class; it does not begin when the professor announces a test. On the first day of class, the professor provides an overview, or outline, of what you will learn. Attend every class. The main points covered in the class will be on the test. Read your assignments a little at a time starting from the first day. If you distribute your practice, you will find it easier to learn and to remember.

When it comes time to review for the test, you will already know what to expect on the test; and you will have learned the material by attending the lectures and reading your text. Reviewing for the test is just review; it is not original learning. It is a chance to strengthen what you have learned so that you can relax and do your best on the test. Review is one of the final steps in learning. With review you will gain a sense of confidence and satisfaction in your studies.

If you are not prepared, you will need to cram for the test and you may not be as successful on the test as you could be. If you are not successful, you may get the mistaken idea that you cannot be successful in college. Cramming for the test produces stress since you will need to learn a great deal of information in a short time. Stress can interfere with memory and cause you to freeze up on exams. It is also difficult to remember if you have to cram. The memory works best if you do a small amount of learning regularly over a period of time. Cramming is hard work and no fun. The worst problem with cramming is that it causes you to dislike education. It is difficult to continue to do something that you have learned to dislike.

Good preparation is the key to success in many areas of life. Whether you are taking a college course, playing a basketball game, going on vacation, planning a wedding, or building a house, good preparation will help to guarantee your success. Begin with your vision of the future and boldly take the first steps. The best preparation for the future is the good use of your time today.

The future starts today, not tomorrow.

—Pope John Paul II

Success over the Internet

Visit the College Success website at www.cuyamaca.edu/collegesuccess/

The College Success website is continually updated with new topics and links to the material presented in this chapter. Topics include

- Tips for taking tests
- Dealing with math anxiety
- How to study for math tests
- How to take math tests
- How to guess on a test
- Test anxiety
- Multiple-choice exams
- Dealing with difficult questions

Contact your instructor if you have any problems accessing the College Success website.

Endnotes

1. G. A. Miller, "The Magical Number Seven, Plus or Minus Two: Some Limits on Our Capacity for Processing Information," *Psychological Review* 63 (March 1956): 81–97.
2. From Aguilar et al., *The Community College: A New Beginning,* 2nd ed. Copyright 1998 by Kendall/Hunt Publishing Company.

Taking Notes, Writing, and Speaking

Chapter 5

Chapter Focus

Read to answer these key questions:

Why is it important to take notes?   What are some good listening techniques?   What are some tips for taking good lecture notes?   What are some note taking systems?   What is the best way to review my notes for the test?   What is power writing?   How can I make a good speech?

Knowing how to listen and take good notes can make your college life easier and may help you in your future career as well. Professionals in many occupations take notes as a way of recording key ideas for later use. Whether you become a journalist, attorney, architect, engineer, or other professional, listening and taking good notes can help you to get ahead in your career.

Good writing and speaking skills are important to your success in college and in your career. In college you will be asked to write term papers and complete other writing assignments. The writing skills you learn in college will be used later in jobs involving high responsibility and good pay. On the job, you will write reports, memos, and proposals. You will probably take a speech class and give oral reports in other classes. On the job, you will present your ideas orally to your colleagues and business associates.

> What is your evaluation of your note taking skills?

Why Take Notes?

The most important reason for taking notes is to remember important material for the test or for future use in your career. If you just attend class without taking notes, you will forget most of the material by the next day.

How does taking notes enhance memory?

- In college, the lecture is a way of supplementing the written material in the textbook. Without good notes, an important part of the course is missing. Note taking provides material to rehearse or recite, so that it can be stored in long-term memory.
- By taking notes and imposing your own organization on them, the notes become more personally meaningful. If they are meaningful, they are easier to remember.

From *College & Career Success*, 3rd edition by Marsha Fralick. Copyright © 2006 by Kendall/Hunt Publishing Company. Reprinted by permission.

- Taking notes helps you to make new connections. New material is remembered by connecting it to what you already know.
- For kinesthetic and tactile learners, the physical act of writing the material is helpful in learning and remembering it.
- For visual learners, notes provide a visual map of the material to be learned.
- For auditory learners, taking notes is a way to listen carefully and record information to be stored in the memory.
- Note taking helps students to concentrate, maintain focus, and stay awake.
- Attending the lectures and taking notes helps you to understand what the professor thinks is important and to know what to study for the exam.

The College Lecture

You will experience many different types of lectures while in college. At larger universities many of the beginning-level courses are taught in large lecture halls with 300 people or more. More advanced courses tend to have fewer students. In large lecture situations, it is not always possible or appropriate to ask questions. Under these circumstances, the large lecture is often supplemented by smaller discussion sessions where you can ask questions and review the lecture material. Although attendance may not be checked, it is important to attend both the lectures and the discussion session.

A formal college lecture is divided into four parts. Understanding these parts will help you to be a good listener and take good notes.

1. **Introduction.** The professor uses the introduction to set the stage and to introduce the topic of the lecture. Often an overview or outline of the lecture is presented. Use the introduction as a way to begin thinking about the organization of your notes and the key ideas you will need to write down.
2. **Thesis.** The thesis is the key idea in the lecture. In a one-hour lecture, there is usually one thesis statement. Listen carefully for the thesis statement and write it down in your notes. Review the thesis statement and related ideas for the exam.
3. **Body.** The body of the lecture usually consists of five or six main ideas with discussion and clarification of each idea. As a note taker, your job is to identify the main ideas, write them in your notes and put in enough of the explanation or examples to understand the key ideas.
4. **Conclusion.** In the conclusion, the professor summarizes the key points of the lecture and sometimes asks for questions. Use the conclusion as an opportunity to check your understanding of the lecture and to ask questions to clarify the key points.

How to Be a Good Listener

Effective note taking begins with good listening. What is good listening? Sometimes students confuse listening with hearing. Hearing is done with the ears. Listening is a more active process done with the ears and the brain engaged. Good listening requires attention and concentration. Practice these ideas for good listening:

Be physically ready. It is difficult to listen to a lecture if you are tired, hungry, or ill. Get enough sleep so that you can stay awake. Eat a balanced diet without too much caffeine or sugar. Take care of your health and participate in an exercise program so that you feel your best.

Prepare a mental framework. Look at the course syllabus to become familiar with the topic of the lecture. Use your textbook to read, or at least survey, the material to be covered in the lecture. If you are familiar with the key concepts from the textbook, you will be able to understand the lecture and know what to write down in your notes. If the material is in your book, there is no need to write it down in your notes.

The more complex the topic, the more important it is for you to read the text first. If you go to the lecture and have no idea what is being discussed, you may be overwhelmed and find it difficult to take notes on material that is totally new to you. Remember that it is easier to remember material if you can connect it to material you already know.

Find a good place to sit. Arrive early to get a good seat. The best seats in the classroom are in the front and center of the room. If you were buying concert tickets, these would be the best and most expensive seats. Find a seat that will help you to hear and focus on the speaker. You may need to find a seat away from your friends to avoid distractions.

Have a positive mental attitude. Convince yourself that the speaker has something important to say and be open to new ideas. This may require you to focus on your goals and to look past some distractions. Maybe the lecturer doesn't have the best speaking voice or you don't like his or her appearance. Focus on what you can learn from the professor rather than outward appearances.

Listen actively to identify the main points. As you are listening to the lecture, ask yourself, "What is the main idea?" In your own words, write the main points down in your notes. Do not try to write down everything the professor says. This will be impossible and unnecessary. Imagine that your mind is a filter and you are actively sorting through the material to find the key ideas and write them down in your notes. Try to identify the key points that will be on the test and write them in your notes.

Stay awake and engaged in learning. The best way to stay awake and focused is to listen actively and take notes. Have a mental debate with the professor. Listen for the main points and the logical connection between ideas. The physical act of writing the notes will help to keep you awake.

Tips for Good Note Taking

Here are some suggestions for taking good notes:

1. Attend all of the lectures. Because many professors do not take attendance, maybe students are tempted to miss class. If you do not attend the lectures, however, you will not know what the professor thinks is important and what to study for the test. There will be important points covered in the lectures that are not in the book.
2. Have the proper materials. A three-ring notebook and notebook paper are recommended. Organize notes chronologically and include any handouts given in class. You can have a small notebook for each class or a single large notebook with dividers for each class. Just take the notebook paper to class and later file it in your notebook at home.
3. Begin your notes by writing the date of the lecture, so you can keep your notes in order.
4. Write notes on the front side only of each piece of paper. This will allow you to spread the pages out and see the big picture or pattern in the lectures when you are reviewing.
5. Write notes neatly and legibly so you can read and review them easily.
6. Do not waste time recopying or typing your notes. Your time would be better spent reviewing your notes.
7. As a general rule, do not rely on a tape recorder for taking notes. With a tape recorder, you will have to listen to the lecture again on tape. For a semester course this would be about forty-five hours of tape! It is much faster to review carefully written notes.

8. Copy down everything written on the board and the main points from transparencies or visual presentations. If it is important enough for the professor to write on the board, it is important enough to be on the test.
9. Use key words and phrases in your notes. Leave out unimportant words and don't worry about grammar.
10. Use abbreviations as long as you can read them. Entire sentences or paragraphs are not necessary and you may not have time to write them.
11. Don't loan your whole notebook to someone else because you may not get it back. If you want to share your notes, make copies.
12. If the professor talks too fast, listen carefully for the key ideas and write them down. Leave spaces in your notes to fill in later. You may be able to find the information in the text or get the information from another student.

Listening and Note Taking

Test what you have learned by selecting the correct answer to the following questions.

1. When taking notes on a college lecture, it is most important to
   A. write down everything you hear.
   B. write down the main ideas and enough explanation to understand them.
   C. write down names, dates, places, and numbers.

2. To be a good listener,
   A. read or skim over the material before you attend the lecture.
   B. attend the lecture first and then read the text.
   C. remember that listening is more important than note taking.

3. To stay awake during the lecture,
   A. drink lots of coffee.
   B. sit near your friends so you can make some comments on the lecture.
   C. listen actively by taking notes.

4. Since attendance is not always checked in college classes,
   A. it is not necessary to attend class if you read the textbook.
   B. it is acceptable to miss lectures as long as you show up for the exams.
   C. it is up to you to attend every class.

5. When taking notes, be sure to
   A. use complete sentences and good grammar.
   B. write down whatever is written on the board or the visual presentations.
   C. write the notes quickly without worrying about neatness.

How did you do on the quiz? Check your answers: 1. B, 2. A, 3. C, 4. C, 5. B

NOTE-TAKING SYSTEMS
–Cornell Format
–Outline Method
–Mind Map

Note–Taking Systems

There are several systems for taking notes. How you take notes will depend on your learning style and the lecturer's speaking style. Experiment with these systems and use what works best for you.

The Cornell Format

The Cornell system is an efficient method of taking notes and reviewing them. It appeals to students who are logical, orderly and organized and lectures that fit into this pattern. The Cornell format is especially helpful for thinking about key points as you review your notes.

Step 1: Prepare. To use the Cornell format, you will need a three-ring notebook with loose-leaf paper. Draw a vertical line 2½ inches from the left side of the paper. This is the recall column that can be used to write key ideas when reviewing. Use the remaining section of the paper for your notes. Write the date and title of the lecture at the top of the page.

The Cornell Format

Date	Title of Lecture
Recall column	Key idea
	Minor point or explanation
	More details
Key words	Key idea
	Details
	Details
	Details
	Key idea
	Details
	Details
	Details

Step 2: Take notes. Use the large area to the right of the recall column to take notes. Listen for key ideas and write them just to the right of the recall column line as in the diagram above. Indent your notes for minor points and illustrative details. Then skip a space and write the next key idea. Don't worry about using numbers or letters as in an outline format. Just use the indentations and spacing to highlight and separate key ideas. Use short phrases, key words, and abbreviations. Complete sentences are not necessary, but write legibly so you can read your notes later.

Step 3: Use the recall column for review. Read over your notes and write down key words or ideas from the lecture in the recall column. Ask yourself, "What is this about?" Cover up the notes on the right-hand side and recite the key ideas of the lecture. Another variation is to write questions in the margin. Find the key ideas and then write possible exam questions in the recall column. Cover your notes and see if you can answer the questions.

The Outline Method

If the lecture is well organized, some students just take notes in outline format. Sometimes lecturers will show their outline as they speak.

- Use Roman numerals to label main topics. Then use capital letters for main ideas and Arabic numerals for related details or examples.
- You can use a free-form outline using just indentation to separate main ideas and supporting details.
- Leave spaces to fill in material later.
- Use a highlighter to review your notes as soon as possible after the lecture.

The Outline Method

Date	Title of Lecture

I. Main Idea
   A. Important Idea
      1. Detail or example
      2. Detail
      3. Detail
   B. Important Idea
      1. Detail
      2. Detail
(Leave space here.)

II. Main Idea
   A. Important Idea
      1. Detail or example
      2. Detail
      3. Detail

The Mind Map

A mind map shows the relationship between ideas in a visual way. It is much easier to remember items that are organized and linked together in a personally meaningful way. As a result, recall and review is quicker and more effective. Mind maps have appeal to visual learners and those who do not want to be limited by a set structure as in the outline formats. They can also be used for lectures that are not highly structured. Here are some suggestions for using the mind-mapping technique:

- Turn your paper sideways to give you more space. Use standard-size notebook paper or consider larger sheets if possible.
- Write the main idea in the center of the page and circle it.

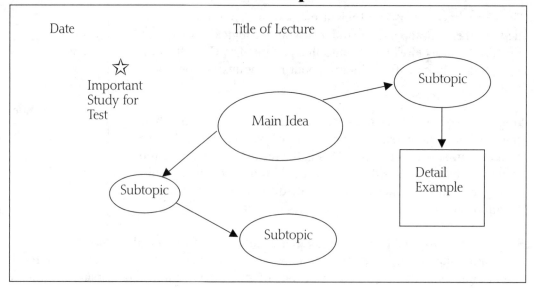

- Arrange ideas so that more important ideas are closer to the center and less important ideas are farther out.
- Show the relationship of the minor points to the main ideas using lines, circles, boxes, charts, and other visual devices. Here is where you can use your creativity and imagination to make a visual picture of the key ideas in the lecture.
- Use symbols and drawings.
- Use different colors to separate main ideas.
- When the lecturer moves to another main idea, start a new mind map.
- When you are done with the lecture, quickly review your mind maps. Add any written material that will be helpful in understanding the map later.
- A mind map can also be used as
    - a review tool for remembering and relating the key ideas in the textbook.
    - a preparation tool for essay exams in which remembering main ideas and relationships are important.
    - the first step in organizing ideas for a term paper.

> What note taking system works best for you?

Improving Note–Taking Efficiency

Improve note-taking efficiency by listening for key words that signal the main ideas and supporting details. Learn to write faster by using telegraphic sentences, abbreviations, and symbols.

Signal Words

Signal words are clues to understanding the structure and content of a lecture. Recognizing signal words can help you identify key ideas and organize them in your notes. The table on the following page lists some common signal words and their meaning.

Signal Words

Type	Examples	Meaning
Main idea words	And most important A major development The basic concept is Remember that The main idea is We will focus on The key is	Introduce the key points that need to be written in your notes.
Example words	To illustrate For example For instance	Clarify and illustrate the main ideas in the lecture. Write these examples in your notes after the main idea. If multiple examples are given, write down the ones you have time for or the ones that you understand the best.
Addition words	In addition Also Furthermore	Add more important information. Write these points down in your notes.
Enumeration words	The five steps First, second, third Next	Signal a list. Write down the list in your notes and number the items.
Time words	Before, after Formerly Subsequently Prior Meanwhile	Signal the order of events. Write down the events in the correct order in your notes.
Cause and effect words	Therefore As a result If . . ., then	Signal important concepts that might be on the exam. When you hear these words, label them "cause" and "effect" in your notes and review these ideas for the exam.
Definition words	In other words It simply means That is In essence	Provide the meanings of words or simplify complex ideas. Write these definitions or clarifications in your notes.
Swivel words	However Nevertheless Yes, but Still	Provide exceptions, qualifications, or further clarification. Write down qualifying comments in your notes.
Compare and contrast words	Similarly Likewise In contrast	Present similarities or differences. Write these similarities and differences in your notes and label them.
Summary words	In conclusion To sum up In a nutshell	Restate the important ideas of the lecture. Write the summaries in your notes.
Test words	This is important. Remember this. You'll see this again. You might want to study this for the test.	Provide a clue that the material will be on the test. Write these down in your notes and mark them in a way that stands out. Put a star or asterisk next to these items or highlight them. Each professor has his or her own test clue words.

Telegraphic Sentences

Telegraphic sentences are short, abbreviated sentences used in note taking. There are four rules for telegraphic sentences:

1. Write key words only.
2. Omit unnecessary words (*a, an, the*)

3. Ignore rules of grammar.
4. Use abbreviations and symbols.

Here is an example of a small part of a lecture followed by a student's telegraphic notes:

Heavy drinking of alcoholic beverages causes students to miss class and to fall behind in schoolwork. College students who are considered binge drinkers are at risk for many alcohol-related problems. Binge drinking is simply drinking too much alcohol at one time. Binge drinking is defined by researchers as men who drink five or more drinks in a row or women who drink four or more drinks in a row. Researchers estimate that two out of five college students (40 percent) are binge drinkers.

Binge drinking—too much alcohol at one time
  Men = 5 in row
  Women = 4

2 out of 5 (40%) college students binge

Abbreviations

If you have time, write out words in their entirety for ease of reading. If you are short on time, use any abbreviation as long as you can read it. Here are some ideas:

1. Use the first syllable of the word.

democracy	dem
education	ed
politics	pol
different	diff
moderate	mod
characteristic	char
develop	dev

2. Use just enough of the word so that you can recognize it.

republican	repub
prescription	prescrip
introduction	intro
intelligence	intell
association	assoc

3. Abbreviate or write out the word the first time, then use an acronym. For example, for the United States Department of Agriculture, abbreviate it as "US Dept of Ag" and then write it as USDA in subsequent references. Other examples:

short-term memory	STM
As soon as possible	ASAP

4. Omit vowels.

background	bkgrnd
problem	prblm
government	gvt

5. Use g in place of ing.

checking	ckg
decreasing	decrg

Symbols

Use common symbols or invent your own to speed up the note-taking process.

Common Symbols Used in Note Taking

Symbol	Meaning	Symbol	Meaning
&	and	B4	before
w	with	BC	because
wo	without	esp	especially
wi	within	diff	difference
<	less than	min	minimum
>	more than	gov	government
@	at	ex	example
/	per	↑	increasing
2	to, two, too	↓	decreasing
∴	therefore	=	equal
vs	versus, against	≠	not equal

> How can you improve your note-taking efficiency?

How to Review Your Notes

Immediate review. Review your notes as soon as possible after the lecture. The most effective review is done immediately or at least within twenty minutes. If you wait until the next day to review, you may already have forgotten much of the information. During the immediate review, fill in any missing or incomplete information. Say the important points to yourself. This begins the process of rehearsal for storing the information in long-term memory.

There are various methods for review depending on your note-taking system:

- For the Cornell format, use the recall column to write in key words or questions. Cover your notes and see if you can recall the main ideas. Place a checkmark by the items you have mastered. Don't worry about mastering all the key points from the beginning. With each review, it will be easier to remember the information.
- For the outline format, use a highlighter to mark the key ideas as you repeat them silently to yourself.
- For mind maps, look over the information and think about the key ideas and their relationships. Fill in additional information or clarification. Highlight important points or relationships with color.

Intermediate review. Set up some time each week for short reviews of your notes and the key points in your textbook from previous weeks. Quickly look over the notes and recite the key points in your mind. These intermediate reviews will help you to master the material and avoid test anxiety.

Test review. Complete a major review as part of your test preparation strategy. As you look through your notes, turn the key ideas into possible test questions and answer them.

Final review. The final review occurs after you have received the results of your test. Ask yourself these questions:

- What percentage of the test questions came from the lecture notes?
- Were you prepared for the exam? Is so, congratulate yourself on a job well done. If not, how can you improve next time?
- Were your notes adequate? If not, what needs to be added or changed?

Note-Taking Efficiency

Test what you have learned by selecting the correct answer to the following questions.

1. Recognizing signal words will help you to
   A. know when the lecture is about to end.
   B. identify the key ideas and organize them in your notes.
   C. know when to pay attention.

2. When taking notes, be sure to
   A. write your notes in complete sentences.
   B. use correct grammar.
   C. use telegraphic sentences.

3. The best time to review your notes is
   A. as soon as possible after the lecture.
   B. within 24 hours.
   C. within one week.

4. Using abbreviations in note taking is
   A. not a good idea.
   B. a good idea as long as you can read them.
   C. makes review difficult.

5. To avoid test anxiety,
   A. review your notes just before the test.
   B. review your notes the week before the test.
   C. review your notes periodically throughout the semester.

How did you do on the quiz? Check your answers: 1. B, 2. C, 3. A, 4. B, 5. C

What is your plan for reviewing your notes?

POWER WRITING
–Prepare
–Organize
–Write
–Edit
–Revise

Power Writing

Effective writing will help you in school, on the job, and in your personal life. Good writing will help you to create quality term papers. The writing skills that you learn in college will be used later in jobs involving high responsibility and good pay. You can become an excellent writer by learning about the steps in POWER writing: Prepare, Organize, Write, Edit and Revise.

Prepare

Plan your time. The first step in writing is to plan your time so that the project can be completed by the due date. Picture this scene: It is the day that the term paper is due. A few students proudly hand in their term papers and are ready to celebrate their accomplishments. Many of the students in the class are absent, and some will never return to the class.

Some of the students look as though they haven't slept the night before. They look stressed and weary. At the front of the class is a line of students wanting to talk with the instructor. The instructor has heard it all before:

- I had my paper all completed and my printer jammed.
- My hard drive crashed and I lost my paper.
- I was driving to school and my paper flew off my motorcycle.
- I had the flu.
- My children were sick.
- I had to take my dog to the vet.
- My dog ate my paper.
- My car broke down and I could not get to the library.
- My grandmother died and I had to go to the funeral.
- My roommate accidentally took my backpack to school.
- I spilled salad dressing on my paper, so I put it in the microwave to dry it out and the writing disappeared!

> **PREPARE**
> –Plan your time
> –Find space and time
> –Choose general topic
> –Gather information
> –Write thesis statement

To avoid being in this uncomfortable and stressful situation, plan ahead. Plan to complete your project at least one week ahead of time so that you can deal with life's emergencies. Life does not always go as planned. You or your children may get sick, or your dog may do strange things to your homework. Your computer may malfunction, leading you to believe it senses stress and malfunctions just to frustrate you even more.

To avoid stress and do your best work, start with the date that the project is due and then think about the steps needed to finish. Write these dates on your calendar or on your list of things to do. Consider all these components:

Project due date: _____

To Do	**By when?**
1. Brainstorm ideas.	_____
2. Choose a topic.	_____
3. Gather information.	_____
4. Write a thesis statement.	_____
5. Write an outline.	_____
6. Write the introduction.	_____
7. Write the first draft.	_____
8. Prepare the bibliography.	_____
9. Edit.	_____
10. Revise.	_____
11. Print and assemble.	_____

Find a space and time. Find a space where you can work. Gather the materials that you will need to write. Generally writing is best done in longer blocks of time. Determine when you will work on your paper and write the time on your schedule. Start right away to avoid panic later.

Choose a general topic. This task will be easy if your topic is already clearly defined by your instructor or your boss at work. Make sure that you have a clear idea of what is required, such as length, format, purpose, and method of citing references and topic. Many times the choice of a topic is left to you. Begin by doing some brainstorming. Think about topics that interest you. Write them down. You may want to focus your attention on brainstorming ideas for five or ten minutes, and then put the project aside and come back to it later. Once you have started the process of thinking about the ideas, your mind will continue to work and you may have some creative inspiration. If inspiration does not come, repeat the brainstorming process.

Gather information. Go to your college library and use the Internet to gather your information. As you begin, you can see what is available, what is interesting to you, and what the current thinking is on your topic. Note the major topics of interest that might be useful to you. Once you have found some interesting material, you will feel motivated to continue your project. As you find information relevant to your topic, make sure to write down the source of your information to use in the bibliography. The bibliography contains information about where you found your material. Write down the author, title of the publication, publisher, place and date of publication. For Internet resources, list the address of the website and the date accessed.

Write the thesis statement. The thesis statement is the key idea in your paper. It provides a direction for you to follow. It is the first step in organizing your work. To write a thesis statement, review the material you have gathered and then ask these questions:

- What is the most important idea?
- What question would I like to ask about it?
- What is my answer?

For example, if I decide to write a paper for my health class on the harmful effects of smoking, I would look at current references on the topic. I might become interested in how the tobacco companies misled the public on the dangers of smoking. I would think about my thesis statement and answer the questions stated above.

- *What is the most important idea?* Smoking is harmful to your health.
- *What question would I like to ask about it?* Did the tobacco companies mislead the public about the health hazards of smoking?
- *What is my answer?* The tobacco companies misled the public about the hazards of smoking in order to protect their business interests.
- *My thesis statement:* Tobacco companies knew that smoking was hazardous to health, but to protect their business interests they deliberately misled the public.

The thesis statement helps to narrow the topic and provide direction for the paper. I can now focus on reference material related to my topic: research on health effects of smoking, congressional testimony relating to regulation of the tobacco industry, and how advertising influences people to smoke.

ORGANIZE
–List related topics
–Arrange in logical order
–Have an organizational structure

Organize

At this point you have many ideas about what to include in your paper, and you have a central focus, your thesis statement. Start to organize your paper by listing the topics that are related to your thesis statement. Here is a list of topics related to my thesis statement about smoking:

- Tobacco companies' awareness that nicotine is addictive
- Minimizing health hazards in tobacco advertisements
- How advertisements encourage people to smoke
- Money earned by the tobacco industry
- Health problems caused by smoking
- Statistics on numbers of people who have health problems or die from smoking

- Regulation of the tobacco industry
- Advertisements aimed at children

Think about the topics and arrange them in logical order. Use an outline, a mind map, a flowchart, or a drawing to think about how you will organize the important topics. Keep in mind that you will need an introduction, a body, and a conclusion. Having an organizational structure will make it easier for you to write because you will not need to wonder what comes next.

Write

WRITE THE FIRST SENTENCE
Begin with the main idea.

WRITE THE INTRODUCTION
This is the road map for the rest of the paper. The introduction includes your thesis statement and establishes the foundation of the paper. It introduces topics that will be discussed in the body of the paper. The introduction should include some interesting points that provide a "hook" to motivate the audience to read your paper. For example, for a paper on the hazards of smoking, you might begin with statistics on how many people suffer from smoking-related illnesses and premature death. Note the large profits earned by the tobacco industry. Then introduce other topics: deception, advertisements, and regulation. The introduction provides a guide or outline of what will follow in the paper.

> **WRITE**
> –First sentence
> –Introduction
> –Body
> –Conclusion
> –References

WRITE THE BODY OF THE PAPER
The body of the paper is divided into paragraphs that discuss the topics that you have introduced. As you write each paragraph, include the main idea and then explain it and give examples. Here are some good tips for writing:

1. Good writing reflects clear thinking. Think about what you want to say and write about it so the reader can understand your point of view.
2. Use clear and concise language. Avoid using too many words or scholarly sounding words that might get in the way of understanding.
3. Don't assume that the audience knows what you are writing about. Provide complete information.
4. Provide examples, stories, and quotes to support your main points. Include your own ideas and experiences.
5. Beware of plagiarism. Plagiarism is copying the work of others without giving them credit. It is illegal and can cause you to receive a failing grade on your project or even get you into legal trouble. You can avoid plagiarism by using quotation marks around an author's words and providing a reference indicating where you found the material. You can also avoid plagiarism by writing about others' ideas in your own words.

WRITE THE CONCLUSION
The conclusion summarizes the topics in the paper and presents your point of view. It makes reference to the introduction and answers the question posed in your thesis statement. It often makes the reader think about the significance of your point and the implications for the future. Make your conclusion interesting and powerful.

INCLUDE REFERENCES
No college paper is complete without references. References may be given in footnotes, endnotes, a list of works cited, or a bibliography. You can use your computer to insert these

references. There are various styles for citing references depending on your subject area. There are computer programs that put your information into the correct style. Ask your instructor which style to use for your particular class or project. Three frequently used styles for citing references are APA, Chicago, and MLA.

1. The American Psychological Association (APA) style is used in psychology and other behavioral sciences. Consult the *Publication Manual of the American Psychological Association*, 5th ed. (Washington, DC: American Psychological Association, 2001). You can find this source online at www.apastyle.org
2. Chicago style is used by many professional writers in a variety of fields. Consult the *Chicago Manual of Style*, 15th ed. (Chicago: University of Chicago Press, 2003). You can find this source online at www.press.uchicago.edu/misc/chicago/cmosfaq/about.html
3. The Modern Language Association (MLA) style is used in English, classical languages, and the humanities. Consult the *MLA Handbook for Writers of Research Papers*, 6th ed. (New York: Modern Language Association, 2003). This source is available online at www.mla.org/style

Each of these styles uses a different format for listing sources but all include the same information. Make sure you write down this information as you collect your reference material. If you forget this step, it is very time-consuming and difficult to find later.

- Author's name
- Title of the book or article
- Publisher
- City where book was published
- Publication date
- Page number (and volume and number if available)

Here are some examples of citations in the APA style:

- Book
  (include author, title, city of publication, publisher, date of publication)
  Fralick, M. *College and Career Success*, 3rd ed., Dubuque, IA; Kendall/Hunt 2006

- Journal article
  (include author, title, name of journal, date, volume and number, pages)
  Fralick, M. "College Success: A Study of Positive and Negative Attrition." *Community College Review,* Spring 1993, *20* (5), 29–36.

- Website
  (include author, date listed or updated, document title of name of website, the URL or website address and the date it was accessed. Include as many of the above items as possible. Methods of citing information in the Internet are still evolving.)
  Fralick, M. (2005, January). "Note Taking." Retrieved April, 2005 from College Success at www.cuyamaca.edu/collegesuccess

SAVE YOUR WORK

As soon as you have written the first paragraph, save it on your computer. Save your work in two places. Save it on your hard drive and on a disk. At the end of each section, save your work again to both of these places. When you are finished, print your work and save a paper copy. In this way, if your hard drive crashes, you will still have your work on a disk. If your disk becomes corrupted, you will still have the paper copy. Following these procedures can save you a lot of headaches. Any writer can tell you stories of lost work because of computer problems, lightning storms, power outages, and other unpredictable events.

PUT IT AWAY FOR A WHILE

The last step in writing the first draft is easy. Put it away for a while and come back to it later. In this way, you can relax and gain some perspective on your work. You will be able to take a more objective look at your work to begin the process of editing and revising.

Writer's Block

Many people who are anxious about writing experience "writer's block." You have writer's block if you find yourself staring at that blank piece of paper or computer screen not knowing how to begin or what to write. Here are some tips for avoiding writer's block.

- **Write freely.** Just write anything about your topic that comes to mind. Don't worry about organization or perfection at this point. Don't censure your ideas. You can always go back to organize and edit later. Free-writing helps you to overcome one of the main causes of writer's block: you think it has to be perfect from the beginning. This expectation of perfection causes anxiety. You freeze up and become unable to write. Perhaps you have past memories of writing where the teacher made many corrections on your paper. Maybe you lack confidence in your writing skills. The only way you will become a better writer is to keep writing and perfecting your writing skills, so to start the writing process, just write what comes to mind. Don't worry how great it is. You can fix it later. Just begin.
- **Use brainstorming if you get stuck.** For five minutes, focus your attention on the topic and write whatever comes to mind. You don't even need to write full sentences; just jot down ideas. If you are really stuck, try working on a different topic or take a break and come back to it later.
- **Realize that it is only the first draft.** It is not the finished product and it does not have to be perfect.
- **Read through your reference materials.** The ideas you find can get your mind working. Also, reading can make you a better writer.
- **Break the assignment up into small parts.** If you find writing difficult, write for five minutes at a time. Do this consistently and you can get used to writing and can complete your paper.
- **Find a good place for writing.** If you are an introvert, look for a quiet place for concentration. If you are an extrovert, go to a restaurant or coffee shop and start your writing.
- **Beware of procrastination.** The more you put off writing, the more anxious you will become and the more difficult the task will be. Make a schedule and stick to it.

> **TIPS TO OVERCOME WRITER'S BLOCK**
> 1. Write freely
> 2. Use brainstorming
> 3. Realize it's a first draft
> 4. Read reference materials
> 5. Break up assignment
> 6. Find a good place to write
> 7. Beware of procrastination

Edit and Revise

The editing and revising stage allows you to take a critical look at what you have written. It takes some courage to do this step. Once people see their ideas in writing, they become attached to them. With careful editing and revising, you can turn in your best work and be proud of your accomplishments. Here are some tips for editing and revising:

1. **Read your paper as if you were the audience.** Pretend that you are the instructor or another person reading your paper. Does every sentence make sense? Did you say what

you meant to say? I have read many papers and wondered what the sentences meant. Read what you have written, and the result will be a more effective paper.

2. **Read paragraph by paragraph.** Does each paragraph have a main idea and supporting details? Do the paragraphs fit logically together? Use the cut-and-paste feature on your computer to move sentences and paragraphs around if needed.

3. **Check your grammar and spelling.** Use the spell check and grammar check on your computer. These tools are helpful, but they are not thorough enough. The spell check will pick up only misspelled words. It will skip words that are spelled correctly but not the intended word, for example, if you use "of" instead of "on" or "their" instead of "there." To find such errors, you need to read your paper after doing a spell check.

4. **Check for language that is biased** in terms of gender, disability, or ethnic group. Use words that are gender neutral. If a book or paper uses only the pronoun "he" or "she," half of the population is left out. You can often avoid sexist language by using the plural form of nouns:

(singular)   The successful student knows *his* values and sets goals for the future.

(plural)   Successful students know *their* values and set goals for the future.

After all, we are trying to make the world a better place, with opportunity for all. Here are some examples of biased language and better alternatives.

Biased Language	Better Alternatives
policeman	police officer
chairman	chair
fireman	fire fighter
draftsman	drafter
mankind	humanity
manmade	handcrafted
housewife	homemaker
crippled persons	persons with disabilities

TIPS FOR EDITING AND REVISING
1. Read your paper objectively
2. Read paragraph by paragraph
3. Check grammar and spelling
4. Check for biased language
5. Have someone else read your paper
6. Review the introduction and conclusion
7. Prepare final copy
8. Prepare title page

5. **Have someone else read your paper.** Ask your reader to check for clarity and meaning. After you have read your paper many times, you do not really see it anymore. If you need assistance in writing, colleges offer tutoring or writing labs where you can get help with editing and revising.

6. **Review your introduction and conclusion.** They should be clear, interesting and concise. The introduction and conclusion are the most powerful parts of your paper.

7. **Prepare the final copy.** Check your instructor's instructions on the format required. If there are no instructions, use the following format:
   - Use double-spacing.
   - Use ten- or twelve-point font.
   - Use one-inch margins on all sides.
   - Use a three-inch top margin on the first page.
   - Single-space footnotes and endnotes.
   - Number your pages.

8. **Prepare the title page.** Center the title of your paper and place it one third of the page from the top. On the bottom third of the page, center your name, the professor's name, the name of the class, and the date.

Final Steps

Make sure you follow instructions about using a folder or cover for your paper. Generally professors dislike bulky folders or notebooks because they are difficult to carry.

Imagine your professor trying to carry fifty notebooks to his or her office! Unless asked to do so, do not use plastic page protectors. Professors like to write comments on papers, and it is extremely difficult to write on papers with page protectors.

Turning your paper in on time is very important. Some professors do not accept late papers. Others subtract points if your paper is late. Put your paper in the car or someplace where you will have to see it before you go to class. **Then reward yourself for a job well done!**

> What is your evaluation of your writing skills?

Effective Public Speaking

You may need to take a speech class in order to graduate from college, and many of your classes will require oral presentations. Being a good speaker can contribute to your success on the job as well. A study done at Stanford University showed that one of the top predictors of success in professional positions was the ability to be a good public speaker.[1] You will need to present information to your boss, your colleagues, and your customers or clients.

Learn to Relax

Whenever I tell students that they will need to take a speech class or make an oral presentation, I see a look of panic on many faces. Good preparation can help you to feel confident about your oral presentation. Professional speaker Lilly Walters believes that you can deal with 75 percent of your anxiety by being well prepared.[2] You can deal with the remaining 25 percent by using some relaxation techniques.

- If you are anxious, admit to yourself that you are anxious. If it is appropriate, as in a beginning speech class, you can even admit to the audience that you are anxious. Once you have admitted that you are anxious, visualize yourself confidently making the speech.
- You do not have to be perfect; it is okay to make mistakes. Making mistakes just shows you are human like the rest of us.
- If you are anxious before your speech, take three to five deep breaths. Breathe in slowly and hold your breath for five seconds, and then breathe out slowly. Focus your mind on your breathing rather than your speech.
- Use positive self-talk to help you to relax. Instead of saying to yourself, "I will look like a fool up there giving the speech," tell yourself, "I can do this" or "It will be okay."
- Once you start speaking, anxiety will generally decline.
- With experience, you will gain confidence in your speaking ability and will be able to relax more easily.

Preparing and Delivering Your Speech

WRITE THE BEGINNING OF THE SPEECH

The beginning includes a statement of your objective and what your speech will be about. It should prepare the audience for what comes next. You can begin your speech with a personal experience, a quote, a news article, or a joke. Jokes can be effective, but they are risky. Try out your joke with your friends to make sure that it is funny. Do not tell jokes that put down other people or groups.

WRITE THE MAIN BODY OF THE SPEECH

The main body of the speech consists of four or five main points. Just as in your term paper, state your main points and then provide details, examples, or stories that illustrate them. As you present the main points of your speech, consider your audience. Your speech will be different depending on whether it is made to a group of high school students, your college classmates, or a group of professionals. You can add interest to your speech by using props, pictures, charts, overhead transparencies, music, or video clips. College students today are increasingly using PowerPoint software to make classroom presentations. If you are planning to enter a professional career, learning how to make PowerPoint presentations will be an asset.

WRITE THE CONCLUSION

In your conclusion, summarize and review the key points of your speech. The conclusion is like the icing on a cake. It should be strong, persuasive, and interesting. Invest some time in your ending statement. It can be a call to action, a recommendation for the future, a quote, or a story.

PRACTICE YOUR SPEECH

Practice your speech until you feel comfortable with it. Prepare a memory system or notes to help you deliver your speech. You will want to make eye contact with your audience, which is difficult if you are trying to read your speech. A memory system useful for delivering speeches is the loci system. Visualize a house, for example: the entryway is the introduction, and each room represents a main point in the speech. Visualize walking into each room and what you will say in each room. Each room can have items that remind you of what you are going to say. At the conclusion, you say good-bye at the door. Another technique is to prepare brief notes or outlines on index cards or sheets of paper. When you are practicing your speech, time it to see how long it is. Keep your speech within the time allowed. Most people tend to speak longer than necessary.

REVIEW THE SETUP

If you are using props, make sure that you have them ready. If you are using equipment, make sure it is available and in working condition. Make arrangements in advance for the equipment you need and, if possible, check to see that it is running properly right before your presentation.

DELIVER THE SPEECH

Wear clothes that make you feel comfortable, but not out of place. Remember to smile and make eye contact with members of the audience. Take a few deep breaths if you are nervous. You will probably be less nervous once you begin. If you make a mistake, keep your sense of humor. I recall the famous chef Julia Childs doing a live television production on how to cook a turkey. As she took the turkey out of the oven, it slipped and landed on the floor right in front of the television cameras. She calmly picked it up and said, "And remember that you are the only one that really knows what goes on in the kitchen." It is one of the shows that made her famous.

What is your evaluation of your public speaking skills?

Writing and Speaking

Test what you have learned by selecting the correct answer to the following questions.

1. To make sure to get your paper done on time,
    A. have someone remind you of the deadline.
    B. write the due date on your calendar and the date for completion of each step.
    C. write your paper just before the due date to increase motivation.

2. The thesis statement is the
    A. most important sentence in each paragraph.
    B. the key idea in the paper.
    C. the summary of the paper.

3. If you have writer's block, it is helpful to
    A. delay writing your paper until you feel relaxed.
    B. make sure that your writing is perfect from the beginning.
    C. begin with brainstorming or free writing.

4. No college paper is complete without
    A. the references.
    B. a professional looking cover.
    C. printing on quality paper.

5. You can deal with most of your anxiety about public speaking by
    A. striving for perfection.
    B. visualizing your anxiety.
    C. being well prepared.

How did you do on the quiz? Check your answers: 1. B, 2. B, 3. C, 4. A, 5. C

Be Selective

Psychologist and philosopher William James said, "The essence of genius is knowing what to overlook."[3] This saying has a variety of meanings. In reading, note taking, marking a college textbook, and writing, it is important to be able to pick out the main points first and then identify the supporting details. Imagine you are trying to put together a jigsaw puzzle. You bought the puzzle at a garage sale and all the pieces are there, but the lid to the box with the picture of the puzzle is missing. It will be very difficult, if not impossible to put this puzzle together. Reading, note taking, marking, and writing are very much like putting a puzzle together. First you will need an understanding of the main ideas and then you can focus on the details.

How can you get the overall picture? When reading, you can get the overall picture by skimming the text. As you skim the text, you get a general outline of what the chapter contains and what you will learn. In note taking, actively listen for the main ideas and write them down in your notes. In marking your text, try to pick out about 20 percent of the most important material and underline or highlight it. In writing, think about what is most important, write your thesis statement, and then provide the supporting details. To select what is most important, be courageous, think, and analyze.

Does this mean that you should forget about the details? No, you will need to know some details too. The supporting details help you to understand and assess the value of the main idea. They help you to understand the relationship between ideas. Being selective means getting the general idea first, and then the details will make sense to you and you will be able to remember them. The main ideas are like scaffolding or a net that holds the details in some kind of framework so you can remember them. If you focus on the details first, you will have no framework or point of reference for remembering them.

Experiment with the idea of being selective in your personal life. If your schedule is impossibly busy, be selective and choose to do the most important or most valuable activities. This takes some thinking and courage too. If your desk drawer is stuffed with odds and ends and you can never find what you are looking for, take everything out and only put back what you need. Recycle, give away, or throw away surplus items around the house. You can take steps toward being a genius by being selective and taking steps to simplify and organize your life and your work.

> How can being selective help you achieve success in college?

Success over the Internet

Visit the College Success website at www.cuyamaca.edu/collegesuccess/

The College Success website is continually updated with new topics and links to the material presented in this chapter. Topics include

- Note taking
- Mind maps
- Memory and note taking
- Telegraphic sentences
- Signal words
- Listening to lectures
- Grammar and style
- Quotes to use in speeches and papers
- The virtual public speaking assistant
- Researching, organizing, and delivering a speech
- Best speeches in history

Contact your instructor if you have any problems accessing the College Success website.

Endnotes

1. T. Allesandra and P. Hunsaker, *Communicating at Work* (New York: Fireside, 1993), 169.
2. Lilly Walters, *Secrets of Successful Speakers: How You Can Motivate, Captivate, and Persuade* (New York: McGraw-Hill), 203.
3. Quoted in Rob Gilbert, ed., *Bits and Pieces,* August 12, 1999, 15.

Career Services

Chapter 6

Meet Your WKU Career Services Center Career Counselor!

College and Academic Major Liaisons

- Adrianne Browning, Career Counselor
  - (1) Regional Campuses
  - (2) University College, Exploratory students (broad emphasis or generally undeclared), and other interdisciplinary majors
  - adrianne.browning@wku.edu
- Lana Kunkel, Assistant Director
  - (1) Gordon Ford College of Business
  - (2) College of Education
  - lana.kunkel@wku.edu
- Elizabeth Heller, Career Counselor
  - (1) Bowling Green Community College
  - (2) Ogden College of Science and Engineering
  - elizabeth.heller@wku.edu
- Tess McKinley, Assistant Director
  - (1) Potter College
  - (2) College of Health and Human Services
  - tess.mckinley@wku.edu

> CALL OR COME IN FOR ASSISTANCE
>
> The WKU Career Services Center
> DUC A230
> (270) 745-3096
> Visit us online:
> www.wku.edu/career

About the WKU Career Services Center

Statement of Purpose

The Career Services Center staff assists students in the following ways:

- We help students to develop and formulate realistic educational and career objectives through the process of self-assessment and career exploration.
- We assist students in gaining work experience prior to graduation in order to enhance their academic course work. This includes general employment, internships, and cooperative education positions.
- We help students acquire skills that are necessary to conduct a successful job search.
- We help students connect with potential employers through our online database, career fairs, and on-campus recruitment.

Our Services Include:

CAREER ADVISING

Career Services offers career counseling for students and alumni to assist each person in gaining self-awareness regarding goals and preferences, and to use that awareness in decision-making related to career planning and professional development. Individual appointments are available to review results of career and personality inventories, to provide assistance in setting career goals, to review majors and occupations that match interests and abilities, and to help students plan for and obtain career-related experience prior to graduation. DISCOVER is a web-based career planning system with online administration and scoring of interest, ability, and values inventories, along with links to research careers and majors.

CAREER FAIRS

The Career Services Center is involved with several career and job fairs each year. These events are opportunities for students to talk with employers and explore their career and major options.

CAREER LIBRARY

The library contains resources pertaining to careers, majors, employers, employment trends, and other related information.

COOPERATIVE EDUCATION/INTERNSHIPS

These are formalized opportunities to explore and/or validate major and career choices by working in various career fields. Earn college credit and be paid for working in a position related to your career and academic interests. Intern/co-op orientation sessions are available by appointment.

JOB SEARCH COUNSELING

The Center's counselors are available to assist students and alumni with the preparation and review of resumes, cover letters, and job application materials. Center staff can assist individuals in locating company/employer information available both in the Center and on the Internet and can provide valuable information regarding job search techniques and strategies. In addition, a counselor can assist you with employment interview preparation and, by appointment, can conduct and critique mock interviews.

JOB VACANCY INFORMATION

Job vacancies and other opportunities for students and alumni are posted and updated daily on our online career and employment management system, **TopJobs**. Those individuals registered with the Center may access listings for full-time, part-time, co-op, volunteer, and other opportunities.

ON–CAMPUS INTERVIEWS

Students and alumni may register with the Center, post their resumes online and schedule interviews with employers recruiting on campus—all through **TopJobs**.

ONLINE CREDENTIALS

A student/alumnus who registers with the Center may upload a resume and other employment credentials online by using our **TopJobs** system portfolio component. Individuals may create multiple versions of their resumes, update resumes at any time, and submit credentials electronically to employers. Employers registered with the Center may use the Internet to search **TopJobs** for potential employees among WKU applicants who have their resumes in the system.

STUDENT COMPUTER LAB

Computers are available to assist students with identifying career interests, researching majors, preparing resumes and cover letters, improving interview skills, researching job openings, locating employers, accessing online job databases, and gathering information on companies. The Center's lab is located in DUC A230.

WEBSITE

Visit us online at http://www.wku.edu/career. The Center has developed extensive reference material, information, and links to career- and academic-major-related topics/resources. View current job vacancy announcements, learn how to prepare a resume, ask counselors questions, and find helpful career advice.

Registering with the Career Services Center

TopJobs Registration

- Visit us online at http://www.wku.edu/topjobs and follow the links for registration.
- Use your WKU student ID and TopJobs password to get logged in.

Advantages

- Receive emails about job openings in your field of study
- Receive information about upcoming Career Services events
- Participate in on-campus interviewing
- Research jobs nationwide
- Receive information about internships and co-ops
- Submit your credentials electronically to potential employers

Career Portfolio

Our TopJobs Career Management System allows you to store your credentials online in an electronic career portfolio.

The following items may be included in your e-career portfolio:

- Career Services Center/TopJobs application

- Professional references
- Multiple versions of your resume
- Unofficial copy of your transcript
- Evaluations (internships or employment)
- Samples of your work
- Transcripts*

*The transcript that may be uploaded to your TopJobs employment portfolio is a **copy** of your official transcript. If the employer is seeking an official transcript, it can be obtained in the Registrar's Office.

If you continue to store your employment portfolio on TopJobs, **it is very important that you continue to update your resume and other information regularly** to provide current information to prospective employers. Remember to include any additional training and experience, as well as your current contact information.

Undecided About a Major or Career?

- First, you're not alone, and it's not that unusual. DON'T PANIC.
- Take advantage of the help that is available to you from the Academic Advising and Retention Center and the Career Services Center.
- Do some self-assessment regarding what you like to do, what you're good at, what comes naturally, and what doesn't. Check out free online self-assessment tools at "LINKS TO HELP YOU GATHER INFORMATION ABOUT YOURSELF," http://www.wku.edu/career/career.htm.
- The DISCOVER Career Planning Program is available, free of charge, to all students enrolled at WKU.
- Research various career paths and learn about the skills and education requirements of those in which you're interested at "LINKS TO HELP GATHER INFORMATION ABOUT CAREERS AND EMPLOYMENT," http://www.wku.edu/career/career.htm and at "What can I do with this major?": www.wku.edu/career/whatmajor.htm.
- Courses that meet Western's **general education requirements** are designed to assist students in gaining a broad educational foundation, and allow exploration of a variety of career fields.
- Review the WKU course catalog and look at the required courses for the majors in which you're interested—are you willing to do what's required and be successful? http://www.wku.edu/coursecatalog/
- Run a "What-If" audit using WKU's iCap program— login to TopNet, then choose Student Services, iCap (Interactive Degree Audit).
- Talk to employers in careers of interest, volunteer in jobs of interest, participate in co-op and internship programs, attend career and job fairs—**GET THE SCOOP ON THE JOB OR AT THE FAIR!**

Student Guide to the DISCOVER Career Planning Program

What Is DISCOVER?

- DISCOVER is a web-based program that offers guidance and information to Western Kentucky University students in making important career and educational decisions. The program *is available free to all admitted WKU students with a WKU ID*, and can be accessed through any Internet connection.

What DISCOVER Offers . . .

- A system to assist with academic major decision-making, career exploration, and career planning
- Access to inventory results that suggest career areas that may be of interest
- A means to explore the Occupations, Majors, and Schools that correspond to inventory results
- Information to assist in preparing resumes and job search credentials
- Tips and information to help users learn about conducting a job search and researching job openings

DISCOVER Program Use Considerations . . .

- *Completing ALL components of the DISCOVER Program takes time.* Fortunately, students may complete one component, inventory, or section at a time, may return to the program as often as desired, and may repeat any component/section they wish to, as often as they wish.
- Work on the program a little at a time, saving all information frequently.
- Once each inventory is completed, DISCOVER lists results and category favorites in a personal Career Portfolio.
- You may wish to use the "Resume Builder" portion of DISCOVER to learn about creating a resume. Then create a "rough draft" resume using Word or another word processing program and make an appointment to have a Career Services Center counselor go over your resume and provide feedback.
- **Make an appointment and meet with a counselor in the Center** for help interpreting DISCOVER Program results and using the results in further occupational exploration, or for help with resume preparation, interviewing assistance, and job seeking.

DISCOVER Career Planning Program
Getting Started

1. Go to http://www.wku.edu/career (Career Services Center web page).
2. Log into TopJobs using your WKU 800 number and CSC password.
   - Your TopJobs homepage appears.
3. Click on the DISCOVER logo or DISCOVER text link.
   - The DISCOVER homepage appears.
4. Click on the "Sign up for DISCOVER" button at the top of the page.
   - The DISCOVER Registration page appears.
5. Enter your **WKU 800 number** and **email address.**
6. Click on the [Get DISCOVER ID] button.
   - "Your DISCOVER ID has been sent to *email address*" appears.
7. Click on the Login tab.
   - "You are now leaving TopJobs" appears.
8. Click on the [OK] button.
   - The Welcome to DISCOVER screen appears.
9. Open another browser window, go to your email account, and open the email regarding DISCOVER. Within the text of the email is your DISCOVER User ID.
   - You may change your ID from within DISCOVER.
10. Enter the DISCOVER User ID sent to your email account.

DISCOVER USER ID:	**DISCOVER PASSWORD:**
_____	_____

11. Leave the password field blank (on this first page).
12. Click on the [Submit] button.
    - The "Choose a Password" screen appears.
13. Enter a password.
14. Reenter the same password.
15. Click on the [Submit] button.
    - The Personal Information screen appears.
16. Enter required information (marked with red asterisks).
17. Click on the [Submit] button.
    - Your DISCOVER homepage appears.

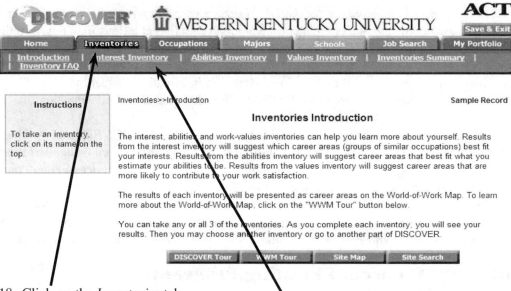

18. Click on the *Inventories* tab.
    - The Inventories Introduction screen appears.
19. Click on the *Interest Inventory* tab.
    - The Interest Inventory screen appears.
20. Click on the [Take Inventory Now] button.
21. Read the instructions.
22. Click on the [Next] button.
23. Begin answering questions (about 10 minutes).
    - The Interest Inventory Results screen appears upon completion.
24. Click on the *Abilities Inventory* tab.
    - The Abilities Inventory screen appears.
25. Click on the [Take Inventory Now] button.
26. Read the instructions.
27. Click on the [Next] button.
28. Begin answering questions (about 10 minutes).
    - The Abilities Inventory Results screen appears upon completion.
29. Click on the *Values Inventory* tab.
    - The Values Inventory screen appears.
30. Click on the [Take Inventory Now] button.
31. Read the instructions.
32. Click on the [Next] button.
33. Begin answering questions (about 10 minutes).
    - The Values Inventory Results screen appears upon completion.
34. Click on the *Inventories Summary* tab to review all three types of results combined.

Keys to Writing an Effective Resume

- ▲ Organize a profile of your qualifications
- ▲ Accentuate your most marketable skills and experiences
- ▲ Use strong verbs
- ▲ Elicit further interest
- ▲ Omit personal pronouns
- ▲ Avoid wordiness
- ▲ Be honest
- ▲ Update regularly

Strong Verbs

The following is a list of strong verbs that you may want to use in your resume. These words are action-oriented and represent skill areas you may have that would be beneficial to the prospective employer. Use past or present tense of the verbs as appropriate.

accomplished	developed	implemented	participated
accelerated	directed	improved	performed
achieved	discovered	increased	planned
budgeted	distributed	initiated	presented
built	earned	instituted	processed
calculated	eliminated	launched	produced
charted	established	maintained	programmed
compiled	evaluated	managed	proposed
completed	exhibited	mastered	recommended
composed	expanded	mediated	reinforced
conducted	expedited	motivated	researched
consolidated	explained	negotiated	reviewed
created	facilitated	observed	scheduled
delegated	formulated	obtained	supervised
delivered	generated	operated	strengthened
demonstrated	handled	organized	updated

Resume Tips

- ▲ **Generally, try to keep the resume within 1–2 pages.** Consider that employers spend about 30–60 seconds initially "scanning" your resume, looking for a good match between you and the job they have available.
- ▲ **Make sure you highlight your background that most closely relates to the skills and experience the employer needs.** Consider the type of job you are seeking and the skills and type of personality characteristics that will be needed on the job to be successful.
- ▲ **Lead with your strongest "selling point,"** which is the background, training, or skills you have that are most closely related to the job requirements. The higher in the resume the information, the more likely it will be read. If you have no related work experience, you might want to lead with your education and the courses that show the skills you're learning that are related to the job.
- ▲ **When talking about your experience, be sure to use short statements with numbers, facts, and figures** that help the employer see the size and scope of activities in which you've been involved (how many customers did you serve, how much inventory did you stock, how many other people did you train, how large was the store, what type of products did you sell, what specific skills did you learn). You want employers to understand what you were involved in so they can accurately assess your work capabilities and "fit" with the job.

- **When describing your experience, use action verbs and career-related "buzz" words** (action: "created," "implemented," "developed," "supervised," etc.). Action verbs help emphasize your active involvement in the experience. "Buzz" words should be used that come directly from the job description, announcement, and/or advertisement. Their use indicates that you have carefully read the information provided by the company/organization and that you are current in your field.
- For ease of reading, **use 12 pt. type or larger in your resume**. White paper is preferred for scanning, copying, and faxing. If you have more than one page, do not staple the pages together, but do include your name and page numbers on the second and higher pages to make sure that your resume stays together when it is in a stack of other resumes.
- Always **list the most recent information first and work backwards** to the least recent.
- Your resume should use consistent format and **should be neat and ERROR-FREE!**
- Be prepared to provide **2–4 names of individuals who are willing to provide a reference for you**. Generally, it's best to provide "professional" references (someone who knows what kind of work you do in the classroom or on the job; a past or present teacher, or past or present employer/supervisor). Be sure to get permission from and help prepare each of your references (copy of resume, job descriptions, company names, etc.).

Sample Resumes
Resume Sample #1
Emphasizing Skills, Honors, & Activities

YOUR NAME
Email address

Temporary Address (until Month, Day, Year): Street Address City, State Zip (Area Code) Phone Number	Permanent Address: Street Address City, State, Zip (Area Code) Phone Number

PROFESSIONAL
OBJECTIVE: Seeking an entry-level position in management.

EDUCATION: **Western Kentucky University, Bowling Green, Kentucky**
- Associate of Arts–Business Management   Anticipated August 2009
- GPA: 3.67

SKILLS:
   LEADERSHIP SKILLS
- Raised sorority's average GPA by .75 points by designing and implementing a new study program while serving as Scholarship Chairman
- Recruited 20 new volunteers in one month for Habitat for Humanity

   INTERPERSONAL COMMUNICATIONS SKILLS
- Developed through serving as a mentor in the Big Brother/Big Sister Program

   SALES / MARKETING SKILLS
- Increased marketing club membership by 15 members in 2008
- Top sales associate at Anne's Boutique in 2008

   COMPUTER SKILLS
- Microsoft Office XP
- Corel WordPerfect Office
- Microsoft Windows XP

EMPLOYMENT
EXPERIENCE:

Anne's Boutique, Sales Associate	August 2007–Present
Starlight Café, Server	June 2006–August 2007
Tom's Bookstore, Sales Associate	June 2003–May 2006

   HONORS:
   Dean's List–2 Semesters
   Community Service Award

   ACTIVITIES:
   Marketing Club–Membership Chairperson
   Gamma Phi Beta Sorority–Scholarship Chairperson
   Habitat for Humanity
   Big Brother/Big Sister Program

   REFERENCES: Available upon request

Sample Resume #2
Emphasizing Employment Experience

YOUR NAME
Email address

Temporary Address (until Month, Day, Year):   Permanent Address:
Street Address   Street Address
City, State Zip   City, State, Zip
(Area Code) Phone Number   (Area Code) Phone Number

PROFESSIONAL
OBJECTIVE: Seeking an entry-level position in business management.

EDUCATION: **Western Kentucky University, Bowling Green, Kentucky**
- Bachelor of Science in Marketing, Anticipated August 2010
- Financed 50% of education through summer and part-time employment.

COMPUTER SKILLS
- Microsoft Office XP, Corel WordPerfect Office, Windows XP

RELEVANT COURSE WORK
- Introduction to Business and Entrepreneurship, Principles of Economics, Management Principles, Consumer Behavior, Business Law and Ethics

EMPLOYMENT
EXPERIENCE: **STUDENT WORKER,** *Western Kentucky University, Bowling Green, KY*
May 2006–Present
- Enter confidential information into database in an accurate and timely manner
- Perform general office duties as needed
  - Schedule appointments
  - Make copies
  - Proof documents

HOSTESS, *Ruby Tuesday, Bowling Green, KY*
September 2004–May 2006
- Greeted customers upon their arrival
- Escorted customers to their seats and took drink orders
- Processed payments as needed
- Charted seating arrangements and communicated customer seating to servers

ACTIVITIES: Dynamic Leadership Institute, Phases I and II
Student Government Association–Ambassador

REFERENCES: Available upon request

Letter Writing

During the job search process, there are many times when it is appropriate to write a letter to an employer. The following are the basic types of letters that you will be sending to employers.

Cover Letter

A cover letter (or letter of application) accompanies your resume. It should market your qualifications and communicate your skills, accomplishments, and potential to the employer. It should also highlight experiences most relevant to the job/employer.

Thank-You Letter

A thank-you letter should be sent to an employer immediately after an interview. Make sure you thank the employer for taking the time to interview you and reinforce your interest in the employer and in that position. Also, mention some of the key assets you have that were covered during the interview. If you forgot to mention something important about yourself at the interview, you can mention it in the thank-you letter.

Application Status Check Letter

If an appropriate amount of time has passed after you have interviewed with an employer, you may send a letter to the employer inquiring about the status of your application. Reiterate your interest in the position and in the organization, remind the employer of your qualifications, and recap the history of your personal contact with the employer. Be sure to thank the employer for their cooperation.

Acceptance Letter

If an employer offers you a position and you accept it, send a letter of acceptance expressing your appreciation for joining the organization. Confirm your date of hire. Also, if you received an offer letter from the employer, you may briefly confirm the terms of employment.

Rejection Letter

If you are not planning on accepting an offer of employment, you should send the employer a letter letting them know that you are declining their offer. Express your appreciation for the offer, and above all, don't burn any bridges!

Sample Cover Letters

▲ Leave a 1" margin on all sides.
▲ Be sure to proof the final version for typographical or grammatical errors.
▲ Always enclose a cover letter when mailing your resume.
▲ Cover letters should be individually typed and signed.
▲ Your cover letter should be brief, usually one page, and follow the general guidelines given above.

Your Address
City, State Zip Code
Date

Contact's Name
Title
Company Name
Address
City, State, Zip Code

Dear Mr./Ms. (Contact's last name):

Your opening paragraph should arouse interest on the part of the reader. Tell why you are writing the letter. Give information to show your specific interest in this company.

Your middle paragraph should create desire. Give details of your background that will show the reader why you should be considered as a candidate. Be as specific as possible about the kind of job you want. Don't make the reader try to guess what you would be interested in.

Refer the reader to your general qualifications on your enclosed resume or other material. Use as much space as needed to tell your story, but keep it brief and to the point.

In your closing paragraph, ask for action. Ask for an appointment suggesting a time when you will be available. A positive request is harder to ignore than a vague hope.

Sincerely yours,

Your Handwritten Signature

Your typed name

Your Address
City, State Zip Code
Date

Mr. Michael Alexander
Director of Human Resources
ABC Retailing
123 Main Street
Townsville, IN 55555

Dear Mr. Alexander:

I learned about your company through the Job Search Manual that I received through the Career Services Center at Western Kentucky University and would like to inquire about employment opportunities in your management training program. I want to work in retail management and am willing to relocate throughout the eastern United States.

I will receive my Bachelor of Science in Management this May. My interest in business started in Junior Achievement while in high school and developed further through a variety of sales and retail positions during college. My internship with a large department store convinced me to pursue a career in retail. The enclosed resume summarizes my other qualifications. When I researched the top retailers in the east, ABC Retailing emerged as having a strong market position, an excellent training program, and a reputation for excellent customer service. In short, you provide the kind of professional retail environment I seek.

Realizing how busy you are, I would appreciate a few minutes of your time. I shall call you during the week of April 21 to discuss employment possibilities. In the meantime, if you need to contact me, my number is 555-555-5555. Please leave a message if I'm not in, and I will return your call as soon as possible. Thank you very much for considering my request.

Sincerely,

Your Handwritten Signature

Your Typed Name

Sample Thank-You Letter

Your Address
City, State, Zip Code
Date

Name of Interviewer
Title of Interviewer
Company Name
Address
City, State Zip Code

Dear Mr./Ms. (Interviewer's last name):

In the first paragraph, state when and where you had your interview and thank the interviewer for his or her time. Reaffirm your interest in the organization.

In the second paragraph, mention something that particularly appeals to you about working for them, and reinforce a point or two in support of your application.

If after the interview you thought of something you wish you had said, the third paragraph of the letter is a good place to bring that up. You can also restate your understanding of the next steps in the hiring process.

In the last paragraph, thank the employer for considering your application and ask for further communication.

Sincerely yours,

Your Handwritten Signature

Your typed name

Your Address
City, State Zip Code
Date

Ms. Angela Chastain
Director of Human Resources
Modern Advertising
345 Center Drive
Centertown, PA 55555

Dear Ms. Chastain:

Thank you for meeting with me last Thursday, August 8, to discuss the position of copywriter at Modern Advertising, Inc. I was quite impressed with the enthusiasm you displayed for your company's future and the helpfulness of your office personnel. Learning about Modern's present media campaign for the Pennsylvania Sausage Company was exciting and demonstrated your creative approach to advertising. Modern Advertising is a company with which I want to be associated.

Your description of the special qualifications needed for this position was especially interesting. My ability to work under pressure and meet tight deadlines has already been proven in the advertising position I held with the <u>Slippery Rock Rocket</u>. As I stated at our meeting, I enjoyed the challenge of a competitive environment in which success is based on achievement.

I would also like to mention that since our meeting, I have received the College Reporter's Award for an article of mine published in the <u>Rocket</u>. This is my first national award, and I am quite encouraged by this approval of my work.

Again, thank you for considering me for the position of copywriter. I look forward to hearing from you soon.

Sincerely,

Your Handwritten Signature

Your typed name

Researching the Employer before Your Interview

Why Should I Research the Employer and Position?

- To gain an idea of the career potential
- To locate employers in my targeted career field(s)
- To gain an understanding of the position requirements and to prepare a resume targeted for a specific employer or position
- To help prepare for an interview with an employer

What Do I Need to Know about an Employer and Position?

At a minimum, make sure that you are familiar with the following aspects of an employer and position:

- Name, location(s), years of existence
- Product lines and/or services
- Parent company and/or subsidiaries
- Financial picture of organization, assets, stock picture, recent mergers, etc.
- Major competitors
- Growth history
- Career possibilities, opportunities for advancement
- Deadline for application
- Required skills and preferred skills for the position
- Specific personality characteristics or personal qualities that may aid in job success

Formulate Intelligent Questions to Ask the Interviewer

1. Please describe a typical day on the job.
2. What do you see as the greatest challenge in this position?
3. What personal qualities, skills, or experience would help someone do well in this position?
4. What are the company's plans for future growth?
5. How do you view this organization as a place to work?
6. What are the typical career paths? What are realistic time frames for advancement?
7. How are employees evaluated and promoted?

Dress Appropriately

Women

- Suit or tailored dress in solid or subtle color, no extreme slits
- No cologne
- Polished closed-toe shoes, basic and dark
- Pumps with medium or low heels
- Nails subtle if polished, clean and not chipped
- Make-up should be minimal
- Clutch or small shoulder bag; choose between an attaché case or a handbag (not both)
- Always wear hosiery and keep color neutral
- Simple and basic jewelry, one ring per hand with the exception of the wedding set

Men

- Navy, charcoal gray, or pinstriped suit
- Shined shoes; tassel loafers, wingtip, or lace-up shoes preferred
- Clean nails
- Conservative, red or navy, striped or solid tie

- Simple and neat
- Solid white shirt
- Avoid flashy cufflinks, rings, or neck chains
- Over-the-calf dark socks
- No strong fragrant cologne

During the Interview

Do

- Give the interviewer a firm handshake.
- Be enthusiastic, confident, courteous, and honest.
- Be aware of your nonverbal behavior.
- Convey interest and knowledge in the position and company.
- Stress willingness, ability, and compatibility.
- Avoid the use of non-sentences such as "umm," "uh," "you know," "well," "like," and "yeah."
- Always present the best of your background or qualifications.
- Listen to the questions carefully and give clear, concise, and thoughtful answers.
- At the close of the interview, establish a date for your next communication.
- Always remember to thank the interviewer for his/her time.

Don't

- Address the interviewer by his/her first name unless invited to do so.
- Let the employer's casual approach fool you—maintain a professional image.
- Dominate the interview or appear arrogant.
- Criticize yourself or discuss your personal problems.
- Speak or act in a nervous manner.
- Ask questions that the interviewer has already answered.
- Interrupt when the interviewer is talking.
- Bring up negative information about past jobs, co-workers, or former employers.
- Smoke or chew gum.

Questions an Interviewer May Ask You

1. Tell me about yourself.
2. What are your short-term and long-term career goals, and how do you plan to achieve them?
3. What are the most important rewards you expect in your career?
4. What do you consider to be your greatest strengths and weaknesses?
5. How has your college experience prepared you for a career?
6. What motivates you to put forth your greatest effort?
7. In what ways do you think you can make a contribution to our organization?
8. What do you know about our organization?
9. Why do you want to obtain a position at our organization?
10. Why did you choose the career for which you are preparing?
11. Why should I hire you?
12. What qualifications do you have that make you think you will be successful?
13. What do you REALLY want to do in life?
14. What do you think it takes to be successful in an organization like ours?
15. How would you define the word "success"?
16. What qualities should a successful manager possess?
17. Do you have a geographical preference? Are you willing to relocate? Travel?

Example Behavioral Interview Questions

1. How have you demonstrated initiative?
2. How have you motivated yourself to complete an assignment or task that you did not want to do?
3. Think about a difficult boss, professor, or other person. What made him or her difficult? How did you successfully interact with this person?
4. Think about a complex project or assignment you have been given. What approach did you take to complete it?
5. Tell me about the riskiest decision that you have made.
6. Can you tell me about an occasion where you needed to work with a group to get a job done?
7. Describe when you or a group that you were a part of were in danger of missing a deadline. What did you do?
8. Tell me about a time when you worked with a person who did things very differently from you. How did you get the job done?
9. Describe your three greatest accomplishments to date.
10. Tell me about a situation when you had to learn something new in a short time. How did you proceed?
11. Can you tell me about a complex problem that you solved? Describe the process you utilized.
12. Tell me about a challenge that you successfully met.
13. Walk me through a situation where you had to do research and analyze the results for one of your classes.
14. What leadership positions have you held? Describe your leadership style.

Section 4

Library and Technology

Library Skills

Chapter 7

Library Skills Component of UCC 175C: University Experience

Course Objectives:

Upon completion of the Library Skills Component, students shall be able to:

1. Identify and know the location of basic library resources, including reference materials, books, and journals.
2. Locate full-text newspaper and journal articles using online library databases.
3. Access the WKU e-courses software (Blackboard) and know how to access the campus computer network.
4. Understand the research process from beginning to end.

Note: The Library Skills Component is part of your University Experience grade. Not completing this portion of the class will severely affect your grade in UCC 175.

What Will I Learn?

Upon completion of this component, students will learn:

- How to get what you need from the library quickly and efficiently.
- How to access information for research papers and projects.
- How to evaluate information resources.
- How to submit assignments to your instructors electronically.
- How to use Blackboard for web-enhanced and online courses.

UCC 175 Library Skills Component Requirements and Assignments:

- View the Virtual Library Tour Video to be shown in class. This assignment is worth 10 points.
- Complete the assignment provided by your instructor involving making a trip to the WKU Helm-Cravens Library Complex and checking out a book. This assignment is worth 10 points.
- Complete the Career Exploration Assignment. This assignment is worth 80 points. **(The details and due date for this project will be announced during your Library Skills Information Session.)**

The Library Skills Component of UCC 175 University Experience is designed to target the following objectives:

- Develop library research skills for retrieving and analyzing information.
- Develop the ability to evaluate information sources.
- Gain knowledge of information technologies available in academic libraries.
- Understand the use of campus technologies and access campus computer network.

Your Library Skills grade will be based on 100 points and will have four components. The grading scale is as follows:

Career Exploration Assignment	80 points
Virtual Library Video	10 points
Topcat Assignment	10 points
Total Points	100

Career Exploration Assignment
Learning to Use the Library

Note: Please read the assignment instructions CAREFULLY and follow the instructions.

Research

Choose an occupation that interests you as a future career. Research the topic using the following information sources as your guide:

a. One book that you accessed using Topcat, WKU's online catalog
b. One journal article that you accessed online through the WKU Libraries web-accessible databases
c. One FREE resource that you accessed online (examples are Google, Yahoo, etc.)
d. The Occupational Outlook Handbook available online at http://www.bls.gov/oco

The Assignment

Prepare a 1- to 2-page typed paper that summarizes the differences between the information sources you have identified and how your perceptions about the career have changed after researching the topic. Which sources were easiest to use and most beneficial? Did they give salary ranges for the career you chose? Did they include educational requirements? What other information was listed in relation to your topic? Do not forget to tell how the information has helped shape your opinion of the career and the choices you will make for the future. Also, list each information source you used to complete this assignment on a **Works Cited Page**.

Papers must be typewritten in 12 point font and be free of grammatical errors and organized following the specifications above. **Students will submit their papers via Blackboard. This assignment is worth 40 points towards a possible 100 points for the Library Skills Component. All papers must include the student's name, UCC 175 section number, and UCC 175 instructor's name.**

Blackboard Instruction

Use the following instructions to access Blackboard:

Step 1

Go to http://ecourses.wku.edu, or from the WKU homepage, click on "Quick Links," then "Blackboard." Then click on the black login button.

Step 2

Log into Blackboard using your WKU email username and password.

> Your username is the first part of your Western email address (the part before @wku.edu).
>
> Examples of a valid username:
>
> John.Smith or John.Smith124 or smithjo
>
> Your default password is the same one you use to access your Western email account.
>
> If you do not know what your Western email address is, or you do not know your email password, go to http://www.wku.edu/accounts/ to find out.
>
> If you have trouble logging into this site, please use the "Forgot Your Password" link.

Step 3

After you have completed the login procedure, you should be able to view all of your Blackboard courses. The Library Skills Component Blackboard site will be included in this area. Click on the Library Skills Master Course.

Step 4

Once you have completed your Career Exploration Assignment, you will be required to submit this assignment through Blackboard. By clicking on the "Assignments" button on the left, you will be able to view the requirements and instructions for this project and also submit the project. Papers should either be saved as a Word document (.doc or .docx) or in rich text format (.rtf). If you have any problems, please contact Sara McCaslin at sara.mccaslin@wku.edu or (270) 745-6103.

Western Kentucky University Libraries Services

To begin your library skills journey, you'll need to know where to start. The Western Kentucky University Libraries are located on the web at http://www.wku.edu/Library/, or just click on "Libraries" on Western's homepage. This will direct you to the University Libraries homepage, where a plethora of information is displayed. You may also visit Helm-Cravens on campus to access the resources described in this information packet.

From the WKU Libraries homepage, you can access the Library's online catalog, known as Topcat, as well as several Library E-Resources (electronic resources), including databases, e-journals, and e-books. The University Libraries also provide undergraduate students with excellent Subject Research Guides for each academic department on WKU's campus. All of these services are accessible from the WKU Libraries homepage, which means you may access this information from anywhere an Internet connection exists (home, work, residence halls, campus computer labs, Helm-Cravens).

Topcat

Topcat is the WKU Libraries online catalog, which is the tool to view the location of the library's print materials, including books, journals, and reserve materials. Topcat is used mostly to search for books within WKU Libraries collections.

- WKU Libraries online catalog
- Located on the WKU Libraries homepage by clicking on "TOPCAT," then "Local Catalog"
- This page displays several different searching options

Once you have entered your search terms, Topcat will provide you with a listing of records. You may click on these records to view each item's Library of Congress call number, title, author, location, and physical description. Use this information to determine if the item is what you need for your projects and research. You may print or email item records for ready reference while searching for the item.

- Records retrieved after searching
- You may choose to view a brief or detailed record
- Detailed records display the following information:
  - Title
  - Author
  - LOC call number
  - Physical description
  - Status (checked out or not checked out)

Web–Accessible Databases

The WKU Libraries provide students, faculty, and staff with a vast amount of digital information. Web-accessible databases are a perfect example of such information. These databases are provided to the campus community via the WKU Libraries homepage by clicking on "Databases (Find Articles and More)." To access these databases, you must indicate whether you are on campus or off campus. If you are in your residence hall or a campus lab, you should click on the "Campus Access" box. If you are accessing the databases off campus, click on the "Off-Campus Login" box. To access the databases off campus, you must log on via a proxy server by entering your WKU email username and password.

Once you have logged in, you will have access to a listing of databases provided by WKU Libraries. These databases can be viewed alphabetically or by subject. Among the many databases provided are Ebscohost, JSTOR, LexisNexis, FirstSearch, WilsonWeb, and many others. You will retrieve mostly journal articles from the WKU Libraries web-accessible databases, and most of these will be full-text, which means you may view articles in their entirety without visiting the library. However, if you find an article of interest that is not available in full-text, you can visit the Periodicals area of the Library to view the print version of the article. One important thing to remember when searching web-accessible databases is that you usually have to indicate during your search whether you desire full-text or just abstracts. Indicating only full-text will save you some time, but will also eliminate valuable information available in print.

Research Guides

These guides are provided to the students via the WKU Libraries homepage by clicking on "Library E-Resources," then "Research Guides." The University Libraries offer a subject research guide for each academic department on campus. The guides include the following information:

1. relevant search terms
2. call number ranges for books
3. listings of databases for articles
4. listings of print resources
5. listing of general reference resources
6. link to department homepage
7. listings of professional societies
8. faculty recommendations

Simply scroll down the web page and locate the department for which you are searching. The Research Guides can be found at the following URL: http://www.wku.edu/library/tip/rsrchguides.html.

TIP (Topper InfoPortal)

This search portal is available to the WKU campus community through the University Libraries. This search tool allows users to find information on a variety of subjects and also provides direct links to the WKU Libraries online catalog and web-accessible databases. Users can also search the web for local, regional, national, and international websites. TIP can be located on the web from the University Libraries homepage and at the following URL: http://www.wku.edu/library/tip/.

Search Strategies

The Subject, Keyword, Author, and Title search strategies below are helpful in determining what the WKU Libraries collections hold. Using these strategies will aid you in finding the best possible materials for your projects and assignments. Use these strategies when searching for materials on Topcat.

Just to clarify, the term "truncate" or "truncation" means "to shorten or cut off."

- Subject Search
  - Enter the subject or topic, omitting all punctuation
  - Truncation on the right is implied

- Keyword Search
  - Enter words and/or phrases
  - Use quotes to search phrases: ex. "world wide web"
  - Use + to mark essential terms: +explorer
  - Use ? to truncate: browser?

- Author Search
  - Enter the author's last name and first name

- Title Search
  - Enter the title of a book, journal, and/or recording

Boolean Searches are considered the best searching strategy. Having the option to search using **AND, OR,** and **NOT** will aid in locating materials relevant to your search topics. For example, if you are trying to find information on cancer but you do not want information on breast cancer, you can apply the Boolean Search phrase "Cancer NOT Breast."

⮞ Boolean Search
- Use AND, OR, NOT to combine search terms
- Use opening and closing parentheses to group search terms: (world wide web)
- Use quotes to search phrases: "world wide web"
- Use ? to truncate: browser?

Below are examples of some Boolean Searches:

Using the **AND** operator will retrieve records in which both terms are present. This is illustrated by the shaded area overlapping between the two circles representing all the records that contain both the word "poverty" and the word "crime." The shaded area represents the records relevant to both poverty and crime.

⮞ Using the Boolean Search with **AND** can look like the image below.
⮞ The image shows that search results will reflect both poverty **AND** crime.

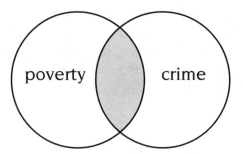

The **OR** operator is most commonly used to search for synonymous terms or concepts and will produce more search results. This searching strategy will retrieve all the unique records containing one of the terms, the other term, or both.

⮞ Using the Boolean Search with **OR** can look like the image below.
⮞ The image shows that search results will reflect all records relating to college **OR** university.

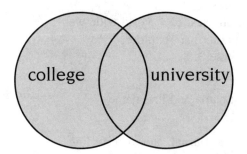

The **NOT** search strategy is used to avoid information related to a search term. This is illustrated by the shaded area with the word "cats" representing all the records containing the word "cats." No records are retrieved in which the word "dogs" appears, even if the word "cats" appears there too. **Note:** Be careful using the **NOT** operator, because the term you do want may be present in an important way in documents that also contain the word you wish to avoid.

- Using the Boolean Search with **NOT** can look like the image below.
- The image shows that search results will reflect only records relating to cats and **NOT** dogs.

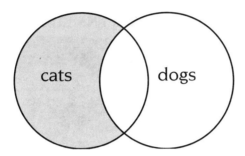

http://topcat2000.wku.edu/cgi-bin/Pwebrecon.cgi?DB=local&PAGE=First

Characteristics of Popular Magazines and Scholarly Journals

	Popular Journal Article	*Scholarly Journal Article*
Purpose:	Report current events Entertain Summarize research of general interest	Report results of research
Audience:	General population	Scholars, researchers, and students in a particular field of study
Authors:	Journalists Often unnamed	Researchers Always named
Characteristics:	Short Pictures, advertisements No citations (sources) Everyday language Not peer-reviewed*	Long (5 pages +) Describes research methodologies Citations Technical or specialized language Peer-reviewed*

*Peer-reviewed articles are those that have been reviewed and accepted for publication in a journal by a selected panel of recognized experts in the field of study covered by that journal.

Plagiarism—Don't Do It!

Students are often tempted to use the work of others as their own, but this is plagiarism; it is against WKU's academic policy and illegal. Students are encouraged to use the ideas of others to enhance their own ideas and thoughts, but it is very important to properly credit the ideas and words of others.

Please be aware that it is now easy for instructors and professors to easily search and find passages from websites used in student papers. The easiest way to avoid plagiarism is to properly cite the words and ideas of others within your papers and projects.

You have committed plagiarism when you:

- Buy or use a term paper written by someone else
- Cut and paste passages from the web, a book, or an article and insert them into your paper without citing them
- Use the words or ideas of another person without citing them
- Paraphrase that person's words without citing them

Library Map

http://www.wku.edu/Library/security/hcfloor.htm

Helm Library

Ground Floor: Government Documents/Law Library

1st Floor: Reference Center/Java City

2nd Floor: Periodicals/ Student Technology Center

Most materials are non-circulating

Cravens Library

1st Floor: Dean's Office

2nd Floor: VPAL (Visual and Performing Arts Library)

3rd Floor: Departmental Offices

4th Floor: Circulation

5th Floor: Stacks

6th Floor: Stacks

7th Floor: Stacks

8th Floor: Stacks

9th Floor: Stacks

Website Evaluation Checklist

Why Evaluate Websites?

No one has judged the quality or accuracy of the information found on the World Wide Web before you came across it, so you must evaluate the information you find. Some websites are created by experts: for example, the WKU Libraries website is authored by librarians who have expertise in the field of information science. The vast majority of WWW sites are designed and authored by non-experts.

Directions:

1. Search the web and choose a site to evaluate.
2. Read each questions and answer carefully.
3. Return this checklist to your instructor.

What is the URL or web address of the website you are evaluating?

What is the title of the website?

Authority and Accuracy

Anyone who knows a little HTML coding and has access to a server can create and load a website. It is important to find out who the author is and what the author's qualifications are in order to determine the credibility and reliability of the information.

Who is the author of the website?
- ☐ I couldn't tell
- ☐ The author is:

What part of the URL (web address) gave you clues about authorship? Check all that apply:

- ☐ .com – a company
- ☐ .edu – an academic institution
- ☐ .gov – a U.S. government agency
- ☐ .mil – a U.S. military site
- ☐ .net – a network of computers
- ☐ .org – a nonprofit organization
- ☐ .uk – a country sponsored site
- ☐ ~/al's – a personal web page
- ☐ Other? Please describe:

What are the qualifications of the author or group that created the site?
- ☐ I couldn't find this information
- ☐ The author's qualifications are:

Purpose and Content

Determine the purpose of the website by looking closely at the content of the information. Some sites provide links to information in the form of "about our organization" or in a "mission statement." This information details the purpose in creating the website, while the purpose of other sites may not be obvious at first. Take time to thoroughly explore a website to determine if the information is subjective (biased or opinionated), objective (factual), or mixed.

What is the purpose of the web page or site? Check all that apply:
- ☐ a personal web page
- ☐ a company or organization website
- ☐ a forum for educational/public service information
- ☐ a forum for scholarly/research information
- ☐ for entertainment
- ☐ an advertisement or electronic commerce
- ☐ a forum for ideas, opinions, or points of view
- ☐ Other? Please explain:

In your own words, briefly describe the purpose of the website:

What does the website provide? Check ONE:
- ☐ Balanced, objective, or factual information
- ☐ Biased, subjective, or opinionated statements

Are the arguments well supported?   ☐ Yes ☐ No
- ☐ Both objective and subjective information
- ☐ I couldn't tell
- ☐ Other? Please explain:

Does the website provide any contact information or means of communicating with the author or webmaster?
- ☐ Yes
- ☐ No

Currency

The currency or regularity of updating information is vital for some types of websites, and not so important for others. For example, websites that provide historical information, such as the presidential papers of George Washington, do not have to be updated as often as sites that provide news stories or stock market information.

When was the website last revised, modified, or updated?
- ☐ I couldn't tell
- ☐ It was updated:

Is currency important to the type of information available on this website?
- ☐ Yes—Please explain:
- ☐ No—Please explain:

Is the site well maintained?
- ☐ I couldn't tell
- ☐ Yes
- ☐ No

Are links broken (Error 404 messages)?
- ☐ I couldn't tell
- ☐ Yes
- ☐ No

Design, Organization, and Ease of Use

Design, organization, and ease of use are important considerations. Websites can be useful sources of information; however, if websites are slow to load and difficult to navigate, their contribution and usefulness in providing information will be lost.

In your opinion, how does the website appear overall? Check all that apply:
- ☐ Well designed and organized
- ☐ Easy to read and navigate
- ☐ Help screens are available
- ☐ A search feature/site map
- ☐ Poorly designed and organized
- ☐ Difficult to read and navigate
- ☐ Help screens are unavailable

Technology Resources

Chapter 8

Chapter Focus

General Resources
TopNet
Blackboard
How Do I . . .

Logging in to Your Course

Your username and password for your online course is tied to your WKU email account, which is automatically generated for you. To find out this username and password, you will need to create a **PIN** in TopNet (our student information system). Accessing your TopNet account is something you will need because you will find online payment, your schedule, your grades, your transcript, your personal information, a place to change your preferred email address, and many other useful tools that we used to stand in line all over campus for.

TopNet

1. Go to http://www.wku.edu
2. Click on Quick Links and then on TopNet (or to topnet.wku.edu)
3. At TopNet, click on TopNet Login.
4. Follow the instructions for logging in the first time.
5. You will be sent to a page to create a new PIN. This is the magic thing that you will need for your email account, so write it down. It should be a minimum of 8 characters. Do not use words from the dictionary. It should include 1 special character.

Webmail (email)

Now that you have that vital piece of information, you can go to WKU Email Account Management Page (http://www.wku.edu/accounts/)

1. Click on "**What's my account username and password?**"
2. Put in your WKU ID number.
3. Put in the PIN that you just created at TopNet.
4. Click Next.

You will see your username and your password. There is a button on the left, **Change Password**, and you should go do this *NOW* because you won't want to do it later. To login to email go to http://webmail.wku.edu and use the username and password you just created.

Now you can go to our course login page. You may reach the login page by going directly to http://bb6app.wku.edu/.

Blackboard

Your **username** is the **first part of your Western email** address (the part before @wku.edu) (ex) John.Smith.

Your password is the same one you use to access your Western email.

After you have successfully logged in, click the dark grey "Courses" button at the top of the screen. Below the heading "Courses in which you are participating" you will see a link to University Experience, click on it.

Navigate around this site and get familiar with it. This site is where homework assignments, grades, class handouts and extra credit will be found.

TopNet Registration 101 Success Tips

Who Is My Academic Advisor? How Can I Find Out?

1. Go to TopNet at http://topnet.wku.edu
2. Click on TopNet Login
3. Enter your user ID (which is your WKU ID number) and your password
4. Click Login, then click Continue Login
5. Click Student Services
6. Click Registration
7. Click View Student Information

On this page you will find your advisor along with your major, academic standing, and expected graduation date.

To find your advisor's phone number, you can look it up online at http:www/wku.edu.

How to Register on TopNet

1. Go to TopNet at http://topnet.wku.edu
2. Click on TopNet Login
3. Enter your user ID (which is your WKU ID number) and your password
4. Click Login then click continue Login
5. Click Registration
6. Click Register/Add/Drop Classes
7. Select term registering for

8. Click Submit
9. Click Class Search
10. Locate class by subject, teacher, times (to view more than one class at a time, hold the CTRL button when clicking each class)
11. Put checkmark in box of class you want
12. Click register
13. Click EXIT to Log out

Blackboard Login

1. Go to http://ecourses.wku.edu
2. Log onto Blackboard using the following information:

    Your **username** is the **first part of your Western email** address (the part before @ wku.edu) (ex) John.Smith.

    Your default password is the same one you use to access your Western email.

3. After you have successfully logged in, click the dark grey "Courses" button at the top of the screen. Below the heading "Courses in which you are participating" you will see a link to University Experience, click on it.
4. Navigate around this site and get familiar with it. This site is where homework assignments, grades, class handouts and extra credit will be found.

Chapter 8

WKU Welcome

Notice: Unauthorized use of WKU computer and networking resources is prohibited. If you log on to this computer system, you acknowledge your awareness of and concurrence with WKU policies on <u>acceptable compute</u> and <u>account retention/termination</u>. Improper use of WKU computing reso may be subject to criminal or civil legal action, as well as University disciplinary action.

This system may be unavailable due to scheduled maintenance between 2:25 AM and 3:30 AM (Cen each morning.

Login to WKU Ecourses

If you have an account on the WKU Ecourses (Blackboard) system, login here.

Username:

Password:

[Login]

Having problems? Read this first.

Your username is the first part of your We email address (the part before @wku.edu). Examples of a valid username: **john.smith** o **john.smith000** or **smithjo**.

Your Blackboard password is the same one to access your Western Email account. If yo know your WKU email address, you can go t <u>Lookup Email page</u> to find it. If you do not kn email password, go to the <u>Reset Password p</u> reset it.

SENDING AN ATTACHMENT ON BLACKBOARD (EMAIL, LETTER, ETC.)

To submit a document as an attachment you could use your email or Blackboard. Please use Mircrosoft Word. (All campus computers have this program.)

1. Log onto Blackboard http://uc101.wku.edu
2. Click the **Courses** button.
3. Choose **University Experience**.
4. On the left side, click on **Student Tools**.
5. From **Student Tools** click on **Student Drop Box**.
6. Click **Add File**.
7. Use the **Browse** buttom to *upload* your paper from your disk (A: drive) or your hard drive (C: drive).
8. In the blank beside **Title** type the title of what you are sending.
9. Now click **Submit**.

If you use anything but **Microsoft Word**, please save your paper as "**RTF**" (**Rich Text Format**). When you save your paper, go to **File** and click on **Save As**. From the **Save As File Type** drop down menu, choose **Rich Text Format**.

How Do I . . .

Find Email Address and Password?

1. From www.wku.edu, click the scroll down bar for more links and select Webmail.
2. Here you should enter your email address and password.
   a. If it is your first time accessing your email, select First Time Users. To look up your email address, you will need your Student ID (800#) and PIN.
   b. If you have forgotten your password, to reset it select First Time Users and to the right select reset password. Once again, you will need your Student ID (800#) and PIN.

Find My Advisor on TopNet?

1. Sign into TopNet using your Student ID and PIN.
2. Once at the Main Menu, select Student Services and then Registration.
3. At the Registration page, select View Student Information and then the term (semester) in which you want to register or see your advisor.

Find My Financial Aid Information?

1. Sign onto TopNet using your Student ID and PIN.
2. Once at the Main Menu, select Student Services and then Financial Aid.
3. Then select Award on the Financial Aid page.
4. On the Award Page, select Account Summary by Term.
5. This will give you a breakdown of cost of attendance, miscellaneous fees, bookstore charges, loans, grants, and other information on billing. Here you will see when a residual amount has posted on your account, charges you have acquired through the bookstore or parking permits, and amount due on your account.

Log Onto Blackboard and View Tutorial?

1. From www.wku.edu select the Blackboard link.
2. Your username and password for Blackboard are your email address (without the @wku.edu) and password.
3. Please note: Not all instructors use Blackboard for their classes; therefore, if you do not have access to Blackboard, it could be because your classes are not using it.
4. Once on the site you will select My Courses and then the course you would like to enter.
5. The following is a link of which you can type into the address line on Internet Explorer to view a Student Tutorial for Blackboard: http://www.wku.edu/infotech/index.php?page=517.

Chapter 8   129